THE ART OF JUDGING

SOCIAL
PHILOSOPHY
& POLICY CENTER

THE ART OF JUDGING

James E. Bond

Transaction Books
New Brunswick (USA) and London (UK)

Published by the Social Philosophy and Policy Center
and by Transaction, Inc. 1987

Library of Congress Cataloging-in-Publication Data

Bond, James Edward, 1943-
    The art of judging.

    (Studies in social philosophy & policy; no. 8)
    1. United States. Supreme Court.   2. Judicial
process — Unites States.   I. Title.   II. Series.
KF8742.B63   1986   347.73'26   86-21952
ISBN 0-912051-13-2   347.30735
ISBN 0-912051-14-0 (pbk.)

Cover Design: Jacky Ahrens

TO CHARLES ROSE

Whose friendship has enriched my family in happy days and sustained it in sad ones.

TABLE OF CONTENTS

INTRODUCTION

On a blustery June afternoon in 1616, an angry King James summoned the Judges of Kings Bench to his palace. Furious that the Judges had decided a case on which he had instructed them to withhold judgment, the King denounced the Judges for their unseemly conduct. It was, he exploded, treason. At that, the Judges fell to their knees and begged his forgiveness. As the Judges cowered at his feet, James asked each in turn what he would do if the King ever again told the Court to withhold its judgment. Each replied that he would do as his King commanded. When at last the King fixed his cold eyes on Lord Chief Justice Coke and asked him what he would do, the trembling Chief Justice lifted his head to his King and whispered: "I should do that which would be fit for a judge to do."[1]

The courage of Coke's reply cost him the Chief Justiceship. Its ambiguity saved his head. Time has vindicated Coke's courage. We are justly proud of an independent judiciary which has so recently demonstrated that even the President rules under—and not above—the law. Time has not clarified the ambiguity, however. Precisely what 'tis fit for a judge to do—particularly a Justice of the Supreme Court—remains a perplexing question.

At the outset, we can identify two popular polar answers to that question. I call these the *impossible dream* and the *recurrent nightmare*.[2] According to the first answer, the judge should determine the meaning of the clause in question by reading the language of the clause. That might be possible in "the lawyer's paradise" where, according to James Bradley Thayer, "all words have a fixed, precisely ascertained meaning...where a lawyer may sit in his chair, inspect the document referred to him, and answer all questions without raising his eyes."[3] The view that judges can invariably determine meaning from language alone is self-evident nonsense—an "impossible dream." Admittedly, the meaning of a few constitutional clauses is apparent from their language. No one would dispute the meaning of the clause which says that each state shall have two senators. The fact that a recent senator was dubbed the senator from Boeing was, I assume, political rhetoric and not a serious argument that every major defense contractor is entitled to its own senator. Similarly, the clause which says that the President must be a natural born citizen is clear. Presumably, no one would argue that "natural born" excludes one delivered by Caesarean section.

Cases involving the meaning of such clauses do not crowd the Court docket. Typically, the Court must decide the meaning of clauses whose language is much less specific and clear. The fourth amendment prohibition against unreasonable searches and seizures does not specify the circumstances in which a search or seizure becomes unreasonable. The sixth amendment, which guarantees the accused the assistance of counsel, does not specify the circumstances under which the accused is entitled to that assistance. The due process clauses of the fifth and fourteenth amendments do not specify what process is, in fact, due. The equal protection clause does not specify those classifications which violate its command. The language of these clauses is simply not dispositive of most cases arising thereunder.

This very lack of specificity and clarity has caused some to argue that the judge can therefore give any meaning he wishes to the clause in question. In this view, the Constitution is an empty bottle into which the Court may pour whatever meaning it wishes. I call this view "the recurrent nightmare." Its implications are frightening. After all, the only justification for the extraordinary discretion which the Court exercises is the belief that it is circumscribed by the law. If that belief be mere myth, then the Justices' discretion is circumscribed only by political realities, and the Justices may decide the meaning of the Constitution on the basis of whim, passion, prejudice or—if they are in a sporting mood—by the flip of a coin. That would be intolerable, and no Justice admits to deciding cases on any such bases.

If the dream is fanciful and the nightmare imagined, what is the real choice? The real choice is between *looking backward* for guidance or *looking forward* for inspiration, between deciding as a *craftsman* or deciding as a *statesman*. What follows is an attempt to demonstrate that the better choice is to look backward for guidance, to decide as a craftsman.

I. The Debate: How Should Justices Interpret the Constitution?

Recently, Attorney General Edwin Meese and Supreme Court Justice William Brennan (1956-   ) squared off against each other, debating the ground rules for constitutional interpretation. Their debate has refocused public attention on the single most important question in American constitutional law: the role of the Supreme Court in the interpretation of the Constitution. Speaking to the American Bar Association, the Attorney General admonished the Justices to mind their own business, which he conceives to be the strict construction of the Constitution.[1] Specifically, he advised the Justices to apply the Constitution as the framers intended. He also extolled judicial restraint, a doctrine that keeps the judicial nose out of executive and legislative business. Justice Brennan rejected the Attorney General's advice in a speech at Georgetown University, describing it as arrant and arrogant nonsense.[2] It was arrogant because no one could divine the original understanding. It was arrant because the framers had not thought about the specific problems which faced the country today. Consequently, the Justice said that he could not rely on the framers' original understanding of the Constitution. Rather, he had to ask what the Constitution "should mean in our time" if "the constitutional ideal of human dignity" was ever to be achieved.

This sharp and much publicized exchange has generated considerable comment. The debate is scarcely new, however. Ever since 1803, when Chief Justice John Marshall (1801-1835) asserted that the Supreme Court could declare congressional acts unconstitutional,[3] critics have regularly denounced the Justices for misconceiving their roles and misinterpreting the Constitution. Exasperated congressional critics have tried to remove errant Justices.[4] Congress has altered the size of the Court, hoping to eliminate their baneful influence.[5] Congress has curbed the appellate jurisdiction of the Court in an effort to prevent the Justices from deciding cases "wrongly."[6] And Presidents have appointed Justices who would decide future cases "correctly."[7] When Justice Oliver Wendell Holmes (1902-1932) described the Court as the quiet at the center of a storm, he described its normal condition. Often assailed for their alleged errors, the Justices have repeatedly reaffirmed that they have final authority to interpret the Constitution.[8]

For over three decades Marshall's nationalist decisions infuriated the Jeffersonians. In case after case, the Marshall Court broadly construed the constitutional grants of power to the three branches of the national government.[9] Those who insisted on a strict construction of national powers complained that the Court had misconstrued the intent of the framers.[10] To the end of his life, Thomas Jefferson himself insisted that the nationalists had ignored the original understanding and thereby corrupted the intended constitutional plan.[11] John Randolph of Virginia accused the nationalists of breaking every promise they had made about the meaning of the Constitution during the ratification debates.[12] In retrospect, one constitutional scholar would conclude: "We are not living under the Constitution of the framers but the Constitution according to the sophistries of John Marshall."[13] The question is thus not whether John Marshall read his nationalist philosophy into the Constitution. He did. The question is whether he was justified.

Marshall's successor, Roger Taney (1836-1864), was criticized as harshly for his strict construction of the Constitution.[14] A Jacksonian Democrat who subscribed to the states' rights philosophy of Jefferson, Taney consistently construed national powers narrowly.[15] When, for example, he declared in the *Dred Scott* case[16] that Congress could not prohibit slavery in the territories, he ignited a firestorm of protest. Critics, reviling Taney as a modern Pontius Pilate, hounded him to a bitter death. Again, the question is not whether Taney read his states' rights philosophy into the Constitution. He did. The question is whether he was justified.

A century later, the Court found itself embroiled in the same controversy. In the midst of the Great Depression, Franklin Roosevelt sought to exercise national power exuberantly. In his first hundred days, Roosevelt proposed and Congress passed legislation that revolutionized the traditional pattern of American government.[17] The Agricultural Adjustment Act, the National Labor Relations Act, and the National Industrial Recovery Act all had a common feature: each created an administrative agency to make and enforce rules governing local transactions and relationships.

The Court initially denied the President and Congress the right to empower these agencies with such far-reaching authority. Believing that the Constitution prohibited the national government from invading the retained rights of the people of the reserved powers of the states, the Court invalidated many New Deal programs.[18] The President in turn denounced the Court for its horse-and-buggy interpretations of the Constitution.[19] In the eyes of their critics the conservative Justices were judicial Neros, content to fiddle constitutional text while the country burned. The question is not whether the Justices read their laissez faire values into the Constitution. They did. The question is whether they were justified.

The post-New Deal Court, dominated by Roosevelt appointees, looked tolerantly upon state regulation of economic activities but scrutinized closely any state regulation of first amendment activities. They so thoroughly revised the Court's jurisprudence that modern constitutional law dates from 1937. Critics accused the Court of reading the Constitution as if it mandated the postwar liberal political agenda. The question is not whether the Justices read their liberal values into the Constitution. They did. The question is whether they were justified.

In the 1960s the Court, dominated by a new generation of liberals under the leadership of Chief Justice Earl Warren (1953-1969), gave the Constitution an egalitarian gloss.[20] Critics accused the Court of distorting the constitutional text in order to promote ends never envisioned by the framers.[21] Among the Court's harshest critics were dissenting Justices who deplored the majority's cavalier disregard for text and history. When a Court majority ordered state legislatures to reapportion themselves on a one man, one vote basis, Justice Felix Frankfurter (1939-1962) exploded:

> The Court today reverses a uniform course of decision established by a dozen cases, including one by which the very claim now sustained was unanimously rejected only five years ago....However desirable and however desired by some among the great political thinkers and framers of our government [representation proportioned to the geographic spread of population] has never been generally practiced....
> It was not the English system, it was not the colonial system, it was not the system chosen for the national government by the Constitution, it was not the system exclusively or even predominantly practiced by the States at the time of adoption of the Fourteenth Amendment, it is not predominantly practiced by the States today.[22]

When the same Court majority ordered local communities to put migrants from other states on their welfare rolls, Justice John Marshall Harlan (1955-1971) demurred:

> Today's decision, it seems to me, reflects to an unusual degree the current notion that this Court possesses a peculiar wisdom all its own whose capacity to lead this Nation out of its present troubles is constrained only by the limits of judicial ingenuity in contriving new constitutional principles to meet each problem as it arises.[23]

As always, the question was not whether the Court had read egalitarianism into the Constitution. It had. The question was whether the Justices were justified.

Today those who applauded the Warren Court's "progressive" interpretations of the Constitution worry that a Reaganized Supreme Court will indulge in "reactionary" interpretations of the Constitution. The Reagan administration has not concealed its intentions: it intends to appoint to the federal bench men and women who believe in judicial restraint and strict construction. Many of these men and women also subscribe to the social agenda of the New Right. Consequently, critics fear that these new Justices will interpret the Constitution as if Jerry Falwell rather than James Madison were its father. The question is not whether the Court could read fundamentalist ideology into the Constitution. It could. The question is whether the Court would be justified.

This two-century-old debate over the appropriate role of the Court has demonstrated one fact: the only enduring, important question in constitutional law is how the Court should interpret the Constitution. Since the turn of the century, for example, the Court has struggled successively with several major substantive questions: the meaning of the due process and equal protection clauses,[24] the meaning of the commerce clause,[25] and the meaning of the first amendment.[26] In each of these disputes, critics within and without the Court have assailed it as much for wrongly deciding as for deciding wrong.[27] In other words, critics have often objected to the Court's deciding the issue at all rather than to the merits of the decision itself.

Indeed, some Justices have even conceded that the majority result reflected wise public policy but nevertheless dissented from the decision because the Court had no authority to decree that policy. Justice Felix Frankfurter made the point poignantly in his dissent in the second *Flag*

Salute case.[28] In that case some school children refused to salute the American flag at the beginning of the school day because the exercise offended their religious convictions. The state, which insisted on the exercise as a means of inculcating patriotism in its young citizens, refused to exempt the youngsters from the exercise. The majority struck down the state statute on the ground that it violated the free exercise clause of the first amendment. Justice Frankfurter responded:

> One who belongs to the most vilified and persecuted minority in history is not likely to be insensible to the freedoms guaranteed by our Constitution. Were my purely personal attitude relevant I should wholeheartedly associate myself with the general libertarian views in the Court's opinion, representing as they do the thought and action of a lifetime. But as judges we are neither Jew nor Gentile, neither Catholic nor agnostic. We owe equal attachment to the Constitution and are equally bound by our judicial obligations whether we derive our citizenship from the earliest or the latest immigrants to these shores. As a member of this Court I am not justified in writing my private notions of policy into the Constitution, no matter how deeply I may cherish them or how mischievous I may deem their disregard.... Of course, patriotism cannot be enforced by the flag salute. But neither can the liberal spirit be enforced by judicial invalidation of illiberal legislation.[29]

For similar reasons, Justice Hugo Black (1937-1971) chided his brethren for overturning a Connecticut birth control statute, which the Court found infringed the right to privacy. "The law," the Justice said, "is every bit as offensive to me as it is to my Brethren...who...hold it unconstitutional. But I cannot subscribe to their conclusion that the evil qualities they see in the law make it unconstitutional."[30] These Justices thus made clear their belief that how the Court decided was as important as what the Court decided.

Indeed, any responsible Justice must always ask first whether the Court has the authority to decide the case before it on the particular ground demanded by the litigants.[31] A Justice is not after all a black-robed Don Quixote who must exhaust himself tilting at injustice. A Justice's oath does not confer upon him a roving commission to do justice. Rather, it obligates him to exercise only that authority conferred upon him by article III and those congressional statutes which properly implement its commands.

Whether the Justice has the authority to decide the case before him on the ground demanded by the litigants is a two-sided question. One side is substantive. It asks: What is the meaning of the clause or clauses upon which the litigant relies? Should the Justices read the clause(s) broadly or narrowly? Conservatively or liberally? In keeping with the original understanding or in light of the needs of the time? The other side is procedural. It asks: Does the Court have authority to decide the case at all? Is there a case or controversy? Do the parties have standing? Is the dispute ripe rather than moot? Will a decision by the Court in fact remedy the injury which the plaintiff alleges?

These two questions are often interwoven with each other because conservatives, who demand fidelity to the original understanding, usually advocate judicial restraint[32] while liberals, who demand sensitivity to the needs of the time, usually advocate judicial activism.[33] The very arguments which justify reliance on the original understanding as a guide to substantive meaning are commonly thought also to justify only a limited judicial role for the Court. Fidelity to the original understanding would dictate judicial restraint, for example, if the framers did not intend for the Court to exercise the power of judicial review or if they intended the Court to exercise that authority only in narrowly defined circumstances. Thus, conservatives frequently question the legitimacy of judicial review[34] and consistently counsel judicial deference to legislative majoritarianism.[35]

On the other hand, the arguments which justify reliance on the perceived needs of the time as a guide to substantive meaning are often invoked to justify a more expansive political role for the Court.[36] Sensitivity to the needs of the times would dictate judicial activism, for example, if the Court were an institution that could effectively promote political, economic, and social change. Not surprisingly, liberal activists have rhapsodized about the peculiar advantages which courts enjoy as agents of change, not the least of which turns out to be their insulation from political pressures.[37] Thus, the dynamics of logical argument, which emphasize consistency, reinforce the relationship between the procedural and substantive arguments.

In fact, the relationship between the substantive and procedural arguments is rather more complex. A Justice who believes himself constrained by the original understanding would give the text a very liberal reading if he concluded that that is what the framers intended.[38] Moreover, a Justice might conceivably conclude that the framers expected the Court to give new meaning to the general clauses of the Constitution in order to "adapt it to the various crises of human affairs."[39]

Thus, fidelity to the original understanding could dictate liberal results
and judicial activism. Contrariwise, a Justice who believes that the
Court is free to decide whatever it wishes may conclude in a particular
case that the Court should stay its hand and refrain from deciding.
Alternatively, a Justice who sensitively balances competing public
policies might conceivably render a conservative decree. Thus, sensitivity to the needs of the time could dictate judicial restraint and conservative results. In other words, there are four rather than two theoretical
approaches to judging. A judicial activist might interpret a substantive
provision broadly (liberally) or narrowly (conservatively). Similarly, an
advocate of judicial restraint might read a substantive provision
broadly (liberally) or narrowly (conservatively).

(PROCEDURE)

	JUDICIAL RESTRAINT	JUDICIAL ACTIVISM
NARROW	Judicial Restraint Narrow	Judicial Activism Narrow
BROAD	Judicial Restraint Broad	Judicial Activism Broad

(SUBSTANCE)

The labels which have been applied to proponents of one or the other
of the two distinct philosophies that have dominated the debate thus
obscure rather than illuminate this complex interaction between
substantive and procedural concerns. Sometimes the labels have
reflected the supposed substantive preferences of their proponents:
"nationalism" versus "states' rights" or "conservative" versus
"liberal." Other times the labels have reflected the procedural prefer-

ences of their proponents: "judicial restraint" versus "judicial activism" or "non-interpretivist" versus "interpretivist."[40] The first set of labels suggests that the judge's ideological preference for a particular result determines his vote. The second set of labels suggests that a judge's conception of his role determines his vote. Unfortunately, none of these labels captures fully the complex procedural and substantive underpinnings of any philosophy about how judges should decide cases.

II. The Choice: Should Justices Act as Statesmen or as Craftsmen?

"Craftsmen" and "statesmen" more accurately describe the different kinds of judges who have served on the Court. For guidance in deciding cases, a judicial craftsman looks primarily to the text of the Constitution and secondarily to the framers' understanding of that text. The pure craftsman sees himself as having little discretion. The choices made by the framers must be his choices, and he simply explicates and applies those choices. Justice Owen Roberts (1930-1945) once described his job in just that way: "[My job is] to lay the article of the Constitution which is invoked beside the statute which is challenged and to decide whether the latter squares with the former."[1] Justice Black, the most famous literalist in the history of the American bench, often talked as if he viewed his job similarly. When asked how he decided cases, he pulled a dogeared copy of the Constitution out of his pocket and replied: "I look in here until I find the answer."[2] In fact the candid craftsman must concede that the text does not provide an answer to every question. Consequently, the craftsman must sometimes look outside the text to the understanding of those who wrote the text.

The craftsman nevertheless devotes considerable attention to the text itself. More likely than the statesman to parse the text, he will often subject it to rigorous analysis under various canons of construction, interpretive presumptions about what draftsmen must have intended their words to mean.[3] He will look to see how a particular word is used elsewhere in the text, for example, and will look askance at any interpretation which renders that or any other word superfluous.

The Court's decision in *Hurtado v. California* (1884)[4] is illustrative. In that case the issue was whether the due process clause of the fourteenth amendment required the state to indict by grand jury. The fifth amendment, which applies only to the national government, does require the national government to indict by grand jury. The fifth amendment also contains a due process guarantee. Consequently, the Court concluded that the fifth amendment due process guarantee could not include the right to a grand jury indictment because such a conclusion would have rendered superfluous the subsequent specification in the very same amendment of a right to a grand jury indictment. The Court then assumed that whenever the framers used the term "due process," they meant the same thing. They thus concluded that the due process clause of the fourteenth amendment could not include a right to a grand jury indictment.

Textual exegesis of this kind is essential, craftsmen believe, because the canons of construction reflect reasonable presumptions about how the framers used words. Morever, the framers were familiar with these canons and therefore must have anticipated that their language would be subjected to such analysis. Indeed, Chief Justice Marshall in his most famous decisions relied repeatedly and heavily on various canons of construction.[5] Since the intent of the framers is the interpretive lodestar for craftsmen, the craftsman invariably begins his search for an answer in the text itself, because it remains the best evidence of the framers' intent even when it is ambiguous.[6]

Unfortunately, the text itself is often ambiguous, as Madison conceded when he said:

> ...[T]he medium through which the conceptions of men are conveyed to each other adds a fresh embarrassment. The use of words is to express ideas. Perspicuity, therefore, requires not only that the ideas should be distinctly formed, but that they should be expressed by words distinctly and exclusively appropriate to them. But no language is so copious as to supply words and phrases for every complex idea, or so correct as not to induce many equivocally denoting different ideas. Hence it must happen that however accurately objects may be discriminated in themselves, and however accurately the discrimination may be considered, the definition of them may be rendered inaccurate by the inaccuracy of the terms in which it is delivered.[7]

Thus, the text does not always provide a definitive answer to the question(s) before the judge. The due process, equal protection, free speech, and antiestablishment clauses are scarcely self-defining in the same way that the clause giving each state two senators is. Precisely because the meaning of the latter clause is clear, disputes about its meaning do not arise. Disputes about the meaning of the other clauses do arise, however, and the text itself may provide no clear resolution.

In such disputes, the craftsman looks to the original understanding that underlay the text. Unfortunately, there is no document called "The Original Understanding" in which the framers explicate the text by saying: "This is what we meant; we did not mean this."[8] Even if there were, the interpretive problem would simply be pushed back one more step as judges tried to figure out what the explications meant. Rather, the craftsman must piece together the original understanding from various sources, many of which are often incomplete, sometimes unreliable, and even occasionally contradictory. For example, sources include the historical milieu in which the Constitution was framed, the philosophical traditions that the framers shared and shaped, the contemporaneous statements of those who drafted the Constitution, and the ratification debates in the thirteen states.[9] Reconstructing the original understanding from such sources is admittedly difficult, but the craftsman does not shrink from the challenge. He has no choice because he insists on construing the Constitution as the framers understood it.

A further difficulty besets the craftsman. The original understanding, once discovered, may provide no more definitive answer than the text itself. The framers necessarily concerned themselves with the problems of an eighteenth-century coastal republic. Two hundred years later, Americans must concern themselves with the problems of a transcontinental welfare state. Not surprisingly, cases involving such concerns raise specific questions which the framers did not even think about, much less try to answer. This was precisely Justice Brennan's complaint in his Georgetown speech—and his justification for ignoring historical evidence about the framers' state of mind.

The craftsman would answer that the Justice has conflated specific intentions with general purposes. If the craftsman cannot identify any specific intentions which the framers had about the problem before him, he invokes the values immanent in the text as a justification for his decision. While his decision is admittedly not dictated by anything the framers said or did, it is consistent with the values that prompted the framers to say and do what they said and did. In effect, the craftsman concedes that the framers did not consider the specific question. He argues only that if they had, they would have decided it in a particular way because the values in which they believed would have dictated that decision. In short, the craftsman's decision furthers the general purposes which animated the framers' specific choices.

The argument is plausible enough. Indeed, discovering the general values or purposes of the framers may be easier than discovering their views on a particular question. The problem is that the values or purposes discovered may be so general as to provide little guidance as to how the framers would have decided the specific question before the Court. Whether, for example, the value of equality, important though it be, is helpful to judges in deciding cases is often doubted.[10] Similarly, the framers' purpose—to devise a government of limited powers—may not be especially helpful in a particular case, since that purpose does not tell the judge how limited the government's powers were to be.[11]

As a practical matter, the craftsman often relies on either precedent or the evolving traditions of the American people as justification for his decision. The craftsman's often uncritical invocation of precedent is puzzling.[12] Where the precedent is an old one, the craftsman may be justified in relying on it. The Court which decided it may have included some who participated in framing the Constitution, or they may have been very familiar with the thinking of the framers. Once the founding period has passed, that justification disappears, however. After that, a craftsman ought to rely on precedent only as it accurately reflects the original understanding, not as independently reliable evidence of the original understanding. As Justice William Rehnquist (1972-   ) has pointedly reminded his colleagues: "...no amount of repetition of historical errors in judicial opinions can make the errors true."[13]

Similarly, the evolving traditions of the American people may shed little light on the original understanding. Again, practices in the period immediately following adoption of the Constitution may reflect the beliefs and values of those who adopted it, as Chief Justice Marshall argued persuasively in the *Bank* case.[14] As decade follows decade, the link between the founding period and contemporary practices becomes less clear, however. Indeed, the very adjective "evolving" suggests that the contemporary practice represents a change from past practice.

Craftsmen nevertheless rely on precedent and evolving traditions when they cannot confidently cite either the text or the original understanding, and they do so for one reason: they instinctively look to the past for guidance.[15] For the craftsman, the past embodies the hard-earned truths of experience, through which the people have come to some collective understanding of the values and principles by which they would govern themselves. In that sense, evolving traditions may simply represent the present generation's application of constitutional values to contemporary problems. Believing that the people themselves possess the ultimate power to interpret the Constitution, the craftsman thus feels that he may justifiably rely on the past because it is the best evidence of the people's interpretation.

By contrast, the judicial statesman looks to the future for inspiration. While statesmen do not discount the importance of doing justice in the particular case before the Court, they emphasize the Court's obligation to articulate a general constitutional framework within which sound public policies may triumph. Where the popular will corresponds with the statesman's judgment, the statesman will strive to "open up" the process, to make the process "more representative," and to insure that the process is "responsive" to the people rather than to special interests.[16] Whether the process thereby created mirrors the process envisioned by the framers is irrelevant.

Where, however, the popular will does not correspond to the statesmen's judgment, they often assume the responsibility themselves for insuring the triumph of some particular public policy. If the legislative and executive branches have proven laggard, for example, the Court may have to decree the policy itself. In these cases the Court sternly issues a "you must" decree. The reapportionment cases illustrate this technique.[17] The Court, having decided that malapportioned legislatures were undesirable, ordered legislatures to reapportion themselves on a one person, one vote basis.

More often, the Court may decline to intervene, deferring to the political branches when they wisely seize the initiative. In the latter context the Court's principal function is to interpret the Constitution as a green light rather than as a red light. The Court's tolerance of most zoning schemes illustrates this technique.[18] Having decided that zoning is a desirable public policy tool, the Court has declined to impose any significant limitations on the legislature's power to interfere with the owner's use of his property.

In some cases, however, the Court must play policeman and say "no" to irresponsible legislators who have acted foolishly. The Court's post-*Roe v. Wade* abortion decisions illustrate this technique.[19] Having decided that abortion on demand is a sound public policy, the Court has repeatedly struck down legislative efforts to circumscribe a woman's exercise of this right.

For the statesman, the questions of whether and how the Court should decide are less matters of reasoned elaboration of constitutional principle than of pragmatic political judgment—though the statesman often cloaks his pragmatic judgment in the rhetoric of principle.[20] In reaching a pragmatic judgment, statesmen draw on very different sources from craftsmen. They are especially interested in facts: "cost" facts, "benefit" facts, "feasibility" facts. Consequently, they often cite empirical studies and expert opinions. Relying on such sources makes sense if one is more interested in the utility of a rule than in its constitutional pedigree. Those who must plan for the future cannot let the past shackle them. Past experience may be helpful, particularly immediate past experience, for it may demonstrate either the feasibility or the unworkability of a particular policy. The more remote the experience, however, the less helpful it is because past conditions differed so much from contemporary conditions that comparisons between the two are meaningless.

Moreover, statesmen exercise a different set of intellectual abilities from craftsmen. Shrewd assessment and keen insight are critical faculties for a statesman. He practices the art of the possible, and he must therefore know how far and how fast he can move the community toward a particular goal. The statesman does not need the skills of a historian or a literary critic. He needs the skills of Machiavelli's Prince, who promotes good by practicing the art of the possible.

For the statesman, like the Prince, such political decisions are both inevitably necessary and invariably desirable. Such decisions are inevitably necessary because resort to the text and the original understanding is futile. The text is ambiguous, and the original understanding is lost or irrelevant. The Constitution is a totem, useful only as a legitimizing device.[21] Precedent and evolving traditions do provide more concrete guidance, but the guidance is usually contradictory. As a practical matter, the judge is free to decide as he wishes because he can almost always support whatever decision he makes with appropriate precedents.[22] Indeed, Professor Paul Brest urges the Court to treat the Constitution itself as a mere precedent which may be followed, distinguished, modified, or even overruled.[23]

If the judge in fact enjoys decisional discretion, he ought to make the "right" decision or the "best" decision he can. The statesman sees the Court as a political institution whose members must adroitly use its power to promote desirable public ends. One noted activist has said that "judicial action only achieves...legitimacy by responding to, indeed by stirring, the deep and durable demand for justice in our society."[24] Reasonable statesmen might differ in a particular case about the desirability of a specific Court action, but all agree that the Court's focus on the public good is invariably desirable. Judge Skelly Wright has said, for example, that "[t]he ultimate test of the Justice's work... must be goodness."[25]

Although the statesman denigrates the determinative value of traditional legal sources, he does not eschew their use. After all, judicial statesmen still feel compelled to explain their decisions in written opinions, and that requirement forces the statesman to conform to prevailing expectations about how judges decide cases.[26] Those expectations generally require that the judge explain his decision as if it were dictated by the law. Consequently, the statesman "plays the game" and invokes text, original understanding, precedent, and evolving traditions as justifications for his decision. One federal judge has said of his activist brethren: "...the judicial activist is all too often seen distributing the contents of the legislator's purse or wielding the executive's sword. All this he does while, of course, dissembling obeisance to the theory of the separation of powers by keeping on his robe."[27] Indeed, the statesman must often mask the real grounds of decision in order to persuade the "unsophisticated" who cling to the "naive" belief that the law cabins the judge's discretion. As a result, the statesman may manipulate traditional legal sources adeptly, and his work product is thus often superficially indistinguishable from the craftsman's.

III. The Importance of the Choice: Does Survival of the Rule of Law Depend on the Style of Judicial Decision Making?

All free societies are built on the same foundation: the rule of law. Justice Samuel Miller's (1862-1890) succinct explanation of that rule is as good today as it was a hundred years ago when he wrote: "No man is so high that he is above the law....All officers of the government are creatures of the law and are bound to obey it."[1] The rule of law does not itself embody any particular set of substantive rules. Rather, it enjoins men to govern according to known, fixed rules of general applicability.[2] Rules must be known (or at least knowable) if people are to be expected to conform to them. Rules, including rules about how rules are changed, must be fixed if people are to be able to plan their lives. Finally, rules must apply generally if people are to be treated fairly.

Most importantly, all public decisions must be demonstrably consistent with these principles. People can demand that officials follow rules only if they are fixed. People can judge whether officials have followed rules only if they are known. People can protect themselves against officials' favoring some and persecuting others only if officials must apply rules evenhandedly to all. In this way the rule of law insures that men will be governed according to fixed and known principles of general applicability rather than by the arbitrary and capricious whims of their fellow men.[3]

The rule of law does not, however, insure that those governing principles will be just. To insure the justness of the principles by which they are governed, a free people must rely on constitutionalism.[4] American constitutionalism has three distinctive features: (1) it rests on popular sovereignty; (2) it restricts the exercise of governmental authority through a written constitution; (3) it empowers courts to enforce those constitutional restrictions. An explanation of these features and their interrelationship is necessary to any understanding of how courts should exercise their authority in a constitutional order dedicated to the rule of law.

Constitutionalism recognizes that the people retain the ultimate authority to decide what should govern them. The Preamble to the Constitution reflects that fundamental tenet when it declares: ''We the People...do ordain and establish this Constitution.'' The delegation of all lawmaking authority to Congress, the branch of government most directly answerable to the people, institutionalizes that tenet. The amendment procedure, which requires that any changes in the Constitution be submitted to the people's representatives in the states for their ratification, reaffirms that tenet.

Constitutionalism restricts governmental authority in three ways. First, it divides governmental authority between the national and state governments. The federal principle was intended to prevent the centralization of all governmental authority.[5] The Constitution further subdivides the authority of the national government into three distinct branches: the legislative, the executive, and the judicial. The separation of powers principle was intended to prevent one body from arrogating all national governmental authority unto itself.[6] Constitutionalism thus tames governmental power by fractionalizing it.

Second, constitutionalism specifies how the governmental powers thus allocated are to be exercised. Many well-known examples will come to mind upon a moment's reflection. Both the Senate and the House must agree before a law may be passed. The President must sign it before it can become law. If he vetos it, it may become law only if each house repasses it by a two-thirds majority. Tax bills must originate in the House. The Senate must advise and consent to treaties. Only the President may nominate judges, but they cannot ascend the bench until the Senate confirms them.

Many of these provisions reflect the checks and balances principle which insures that one branch of the national government cannot act without the cooperation of another branch. The checks and balances principle supplements the separation of powers principle and serves the same end. Justice Louis Brandeis (1916-1939) recognized this point a half century ago:

> The doctrine of the separation of powers was adopted by the Convention of 1787, not to promote efficiency but to preclude the exercise of

arbitrary power. The purpose was, not to avoid friction, but, by means of the inevitable friction incident to the distribution of the governmental powers among three departments, to save the people from autocracy.[7]

Additionally, the checks and balances principle precludes precipitate action and induces compromise. Thus, constitutionalism further tames governmental power by requiring that the government follow regularized procedures which insure wide participation and thorough consideration before decisions are made.

Third, constitutionalism flatly prohibits the exercise of authority in some circumstances. Again, many examples come immediately to mind. Congress cannot make any law that prohibits free speech or abridges the free exercise of religion. Congress cannot pass ex post facto laws or bills of attainder. States may not impair the obligations of contract. The government cannot suspend the writ of habeas corpus except in public emergencies. Policemen can neither conduct unreasonable searches and seizures nor compel a person to incriminate himself. Government officials may not deprive a citizen of his property, liberty, or life without due process of law. More specifically, the government cannot take property for a public purpose unless it pays just compensation. Constitutionalism thus further tames government power by setting explicit limits on its exercise.[8]

The framers, astute students of human nature, understood that these mere parchment barriers would never themselves prevent the arrogation and exercise of tyrannical authority.[9] The framers knew that the rule of law inevitably depended upon the rule of men and that these same men could easily subvert the three chief constitutional restrictions on governmental authority. By setting men against men in the political process, the framers hoped to insure that the rule of men would conform to the constitutional restrictions and reinforce the rule of law.[10] In effect, the constitutional restrictions created in those who served in both levels of government and in each branch of the national government a vested interest in seeing that those in the other level and in the other branches observed the constitutional restrictions.

To maximize further the possibility that government officials would respect the constitutional restrictions and uphold the rule of law, the framers created a Supreme Court to police the constitutional system. This last strategic device had at least one important advantage as a bulwark of both constitutionalism and the rule of law. Courts are open to all persons. Any individual who feels himself aggrieved may go into court and demand that the person who he alleges has injured him answer. Thus, the most lowly citizen can drag an errant government official into court and ask him to demonstrate that he had the authority to act and that he exercised that authority lawfully. Justice Joseph Story (1811-1845) made the point 175 years ago:

> For the executive department of the government, this court entertain the most entire respect; and amidst the multiplicity of cares in that department, it may, without any violation of decorum, be presumed, that sometimes there may be an inaccurate construction of a law. It is our duty to expound the laws as we find them in the records of state; and we cannot, when called upon by the citizens of the country, refuse our opinion, however it may differ from that of very great authorities.[11]

In this way a court serves as a forum through which an individual may insist that the officials recognize his sovereign right to be governed by law rather than by men.

This strategic choice was nevertheless problematic. Judges are men, too, after all; and the framers recognized the possibility that they might also become corrupt. The framers therefore adopted provisions that simultaneously insulated the courts from and subjected them to political pressure. The insulating provisions—the guarantees of life tenure and no reduction in salary while in office—would give a court the courage to stand against the political branches. The subjecting provisions—impeachment and restriction of court jurisdiction—would give the political branches the power to rein in a wayward court. The framers could only hope that the interaction between these "odd couple" provisions would produce a judiciary that was simultaneously independent and responsible.

History suggests, however, that these provisions have been largely ineffectual. No Supreme Court Justice has ever been removed. New Justices have often disappointed the Presidents who appointed them. Congress has rarely limited the Court's jurisdiction. Even Franklin Roosevelt at the height of his power could not convince Congress to pack the Court. At the same time the Court has been accused of following the election returns.

Far more important in determining the independence and responsibility of the judiciary has been the Court's own sense of its appropriate role in the constitutional order. Sometimes it has shamelessly bowed to political pressure. Perhaps the most famous such instance was the Court's abrupt about-face after Roosevelt's sweeping reelection in 1936 and his subsequent proposal to pack the Court. Throughout the early thirties the Court had repeatedly rebuffed Roosevelt's effort to extend the authority of the national government. However, in a series of cases decided in the spring of 1937 the Court reversed itself and acquiesced in the President's assertion of broad federal power over the national economy.[12] Chief Justice Charles Evans Hughes (1910-1916; 1930-1941) was so anxious to wave the white flag of surrender in these cases that he became very impatient with the dissenters, who completed their opinions leisurely.[13]

At other times the Court has stood against the popular tide and forced the government to respect constitutional restrictions and the rights of the people. For example, in an early Marshall opinion the Court refused to permit a state to tax the hated National Bank, widely blamed for the then current recession.[14] Later, the Court invalidated a state law that prohibited blacks from serving on juries even though most people in the state abhorred blacks.[15] In many modern free speech cases the Court has ordered local authorities to protect unpopular speakers whose ideas the community detests.[16]

Sometimes the Court has enforced the law even though the Justices disagreed with the policies embodied in it. Justice Frankfurter once intimated that the Court occasionally had to hold its nose. "To say that a statute is constitutional," he sniffed, "is no great compliment."[17] Other times the Court has ignored the law because it disliked the policies embodied therein. Indeed, the modern Court has occasionally revised the constitutional standards by which it measures state law in order to protect the northern press or civil rights groups from hostile state action whose underlying motivations were repugnant to the Justices.[18] In every case, the chief constraint on the Court was necessarily its own sense of independence and responsibility.

From this same history one further lesson emerges: only judges who act as craftsmen can preserve constitutionalism and insure the triumph of the rule of law. Since the Court is not answerable to the people, its statesmanlike dictations violate a fundamental premise of constitutionalism: that the people retain ultimate authority to determine the substantive law that governs them. Were the Court to act as a Council of Platonic Guardians, it would become the source of all law. The possibility that nine life-tenured persons might possess such authority is antithetical to constitutionalism. Yet very long ago Bishop Hoadly recognized that possibility when he declared that "he who hath the power to interpret the law is truly the lawgiver."[19] The interpreter is indeed the lawgiver if he acts as a statesman because he substitutes his judgment about what the law should be for that of the people or that of their elected officials. Judges who play statesman thus deprive the people of their ultimate authority to determine the law that governs them.

An interpreter who acts as a craftsman does not become a lawgiver, however. The craftsman respects the fundamental premise of constitutionalism. He applies the law as the people embodied it in the Constitution or in the enactments of those institutions and persons authorized to make them. Chief Justice John Marshall himself said that "[c]ourts are the mere instruments of the law, and can will nothing."[20]

Moreover, the craftsman insures respect for all the other tenets of constitutionalism. While he does not substitute his judgment for that of elected officials, the craftsman does insist that officials make their decisions in accordance with constitutional and other requirements. Persons who believe that they have been injured by the government's failure to observe required procedures may petition the courts for relief. In such a case where a court decides in favor of the individual and against the government, the court simply insists that the government play according to the rules that the people demanded when they ratified the Constitution.

The craftsman also reviews official decisions to see if they violate any of the substantive prohibitions found in the Constitution. Persons who believe that the government has violated their constitutionally protected rights may resort to courts for relief. In such a case where a court decides in favor of the individual and against the government, the court simply insists that the government respect those individual rights which the people recognized as inviolable when they ratified the Constitution on the condition that a Bill of Rights be added.

IV. A Case Study in Mixed Judicial Styles of Decision Making: Can Justices Act as Both Statesmen and Craftsmen?

A concrete example will illustrate how a court of craftsmen can preserve constitutionalism and insure the triumph of the rule of law. The example will also demonstrate that while statesmen may make choices that craftsmen cannot, statesmen may also choose the same result craftsmen discover. Moreover, the example will show how justices may either mix the two interpretive strategies or use one to reach the result and the other to justify it.

On April 8, 1952, President Truman seized American steel mills and ordered their presidents to operate them as managers for the United States. The mills would otherwise have become idle because the steelworkers and steel companies could not agree on a new employment contract, and the steelworkers had given notice that they were walking off the job until they got the contract they wanted. By the time the President seized the steel mills, the dispute had already lasted many months, meditation efforts had failed, and there was little prospect that the workers and owners would settle their differences soon.[1]

The President believed that any strike would endanger the country. American soldiers were then fighting in Korea. Additionally, the United States had entered into a series of treaties, obliging America to defend the rest of the free world from any communist attack. All these tasks required steel and steel products. The President worried that American boys might die in Korean foxholes because they did not have bullets, and that American tanks in Germany might rust because their mechanics did not have spare parts to repair them. Consequently, the President seized the steel mills.[2]

The companies complied with the President's order but immediately sought an injunction against its enforcement. Although arguments were heard initially in the federal court for the Southern District of New York, the case quickly reached the Supreme Court.[3] The legal issue before the Court was clear: did the President have the authority to seize the steel mills; and if he did, had he effected that seizure lawfully? The Court could have answered that question as statesmen or as craftsmen.

Acting as statesmen, they might either have sustained the President's seizure order or affirmed the injunction against him, depending on their independent assessment of the necessity and desirability of the seizure. As statesmen, the Justices would have wanted to know a lot of facts. How much and what kind of steel was held in inventory? How much and what kind of steel would be needed to continue reconstruction in Europe and sustain the armed forces in Korea and elsewhere? Were there alternative foreign sources of steel? How long would a strike likely last? In short, was the seizure necessary?

Many of the facts sought would have been difficult to determine. Would use of these alternative sources permanently weaken the American steel industry? What would be the consequences of a failure to supply steel and/or steel products for specified periods of time? How soon would European recovery collapse and communist parties seize power there? How soon would United Nations troops die in the trenches for want of ammunition, and how soon would the surviving forces therefore have to withdraw or surrender?

Speculative as the answers to these inquiries would be, the answers to other relevant inquiries would require an even more speculative weighing of imponderables. What would be the effect of any decision on the future of labor-management relations? What would be the effect of any decision on the balance of political forces in the country? Would a decision for the President insure effective and efficient government in future crises, or would it facilitate the President's exercise of authoritarian power in future crises? Would a decision to sustain the injunction subject the Court to political reprisal, or would it force all parties to work out a solution in the political process?

Finally, statesmen might consider the merits of the underlying claims. Were the workers' claims reasonable and fair, or greedy and rapacious? Were the companies' claims responsible and in the public interest, or were they irresponsible and selfish? In short, was the seizure desirable?

These questions suggest the breadth of considerations that statesmen must ponder in deciding questions of public policy. Some are technical; some, pragmatic; some, philosophical. Almost all are speculative. And all were relevant to deciding the necessity and desirability of seizing the steel mills.

Several of the Justices who wrote opinions in the *Steel Seizure* case expressed these statesmenlike concerns. Chief Justice Fred Vinson (1946-1953), who would have upheld the President's seizure order, speculated at great length about the unfortunate consequences of any strike.[4] Throughout his opinion a single refrain echoed: the President's seizure order should be upheld because the President correctly determined that a strike would imperil national security. The Chief worried: "...our soldiers and our allies will hardly be cheered with the assurance that the ammunition upon which their lives depend will be forthcoming—'sooner or later,' or, in other words, 'too little and too late.'"[5] Of course, not all statesmen would agree with that conclusion. Justice Robert Jackson (1941-1954), who voted to affirm the district court judge's injunction, reminded his Chief:

> The opinions of judges, no less than executives and publicists, often suffer the infirmity of confusing the issue of a power's validity with the cause it is invoked to promote, of confounding the permanent executive office with its temporary occupant. The tendency is strong to emphasize transient results upon policies—such as wages or stabilization—and lose sight of enduring consequences upon the balanced power structure of our Republic.[6]

The latter consideration—the effect of a decision on the future balance of power as between the President and Congress—is no less a statesman's concern. Thus, Justice Jackson explored the practices of modern nations in national emergencies, noting that "[t]heir experience with emergency powers may not be irrelevant to the argument here that we should say that the Executive, of his own volition, can invest himself with undefined emergency powers."[7] He concluded his exploration with this assessment:

> ...emergency powers are consistent with free government only when their control is lodged elsewhere than in the Executive who exercises them. That is the safeguard that would be nullified by our adoption of the "inherent powers" formula. Nothing in my experience convinces

me that such risks are warranted by any real necessity, although such powers would, of course, be an executive convenience.[8]

Whether one agrees or disagrees with Justice Jackson's assessment, it is admittedly rooted in his evaluation of many imponderables rather than in any filiation of the original understanding.

Justice Tom Clark (1949-1967), who joined Jackson in affirming the district court injunction in this case, nevertheless reached a different conclusion on this particular concern of the statesmen. Justice Clark thought that the President needed extensive authority "in times of grave and imperative national emergency." Several members of the Court—including Justice Jackson—had previously served as Attorney General, and in that position they had argued that the President enjoyed broad emergency powers. Thus, Justice Clark added: "I am of the conviction that those who have had the gratifying experience of being the President's lawyer have [described his authority as 'residual,' 'inherent,' 'moral,' 'implied,' 'aggregate,' 'emergency'] only with the utmost of sincerity and the highest of purpose."[9] The fact that such advocates may have believed passionately in the need for such power does not disguise the fact that they based their belief on public policy rather than on text or original understanding.

Justice William Douglas (1939-1975) even adverted to the underlying merits in his brief opinion. Perhaps he hoped thereby to forestall any criticism that his vote to affirm the district court injunction was probusiness and antiunion. After all, the President in his message to Congress had left little doubt that in his view the demands of the steel industry for price increases were "exorbitant" and that the steelworkers had made a substantial "effort to reach an orderly settlement of their differences with management."[10] To avoid any such stigma, Justice Douglas felt compelled to append this explanation:

> Today a kindly President uses the seizure power to effect a wage increase and to keep the steel furnaces in production. Yet tomorrow another President might use the same power to prevent a wage increase, to curb trade-unionists, to regiment labor as oppressively as industry thinks it has been regimented by this seizure.[11]

Naturally, the merits of this dispute greatly interested the public in general and statesmen in particular. Whether viewed in isolation or as but one example of modern labor-management strife, this dispute posed the most challenging questions of national labor policy.

Rather than deciding the case as statesmen, the Justices could have decided it as craftsmen. In that event, the Justices would have asked only whether the President had the authority to seize the steel mills; and if he did, whether he had effected the seizure lawfully. Whether the seizure was either necessary or desirable would have been irrelevant. Justice Douglas stated the point succinctly, although he probably invoked it as a rhetorical cloak to conceal his statesman's will: "We therefore cannot decide this case by determining which branch of government can deal most expeditiously with the present crisis. The answer must depend on the allocation of powers under the Constitution."[12] Presumably, the Constitution permits many unnecessary and undesirable public policy decisions.

Though the only permissible initial inquiry for the craftsmen was whether the President could seize the mills, the answer was neither readily apparent nor easily found. Craftsmen would look first to the Constitution to see if it gave the President authority to seize the mills. Article II defines the executive power. First, it vests "the executive power...in a President of the United States of America." Arguably, the authority to seize the mills might inhere in the executive power itself.

Certainly, President Teddy Roosevelt's stewardship theory of the presidency would support that broad construction of the executive power clause.[13] However, the theory that the President can do anything which he believes will promote the welfare of the country unless it is expressly forbidden contradicts the constitutional theory of a limited government of delegated powers. Under that theory the President, no less than the Congress, may exercise only those powers specifically granted. Justice Jackson exploded the contention that the President possessed unlimited executive power under the vesting clause with a gentle needle. "If that be true," he said, "it is difficult to see why the forefathers bothered to add several specific items, including some trifling ones."[14] One of the most basic canons of construction—that words not be interpreted so as to render other words mere surplusage—thus negatived the argument that the text of the vesting clause gave the President the power to seize the steel mills.

Two other more specific article II grants were arguably relevant. One grant empowers the President to execute the laws faithfully. The other empowers him to act as commander-in-chief. Either individually or in combination these grants might have given the President the authority to seize the steel mills.[15] The majority rejected the claim that the President's powers as commander-in-chief included the power to seize private property to keep labor disputes from stopping production. Admittedly, the text did not explicitly authorize the seizure. In Justice Jackson's view, the Constitution, read as a whole, refuted the claim. As the Justice pointed out: "His command power is not such an absolute as might be implied from that office in a militaristic system but is subject to limitations consistent with a constitutional Republic whose law and policy-making branch is a representative Congress."[16] He explained that the text conferred substantial war powers on the Congress. He concluded:

> Such a limitation on the command power, written at a time when the militia rather than a standing army was contemplated as the military weapon of the Republic, underscores the Constitution's policy that Congress, not the Executive, should control utilization of the war power as an instrument of domestic policy.[17]

Similarly, the faithful execution clause did not explicitly authorize the presidential seizure. Again, Justice Jackson sought to resolve the textual ambiguity of the grant by looking to other parts of the Constitution. He focused on the fifth amendment:

> That authority [to execute the laws faithfully] must be matched against words of the Fifth Amendment that "No person shall be...deprived of life, liberty or property, without due process of law...." One gives a governmental authority that reaches so far as there is law, the other gives a private right that authority shall go no farther. These signify about all there is of the principle that ours is a government of laws, not of men, and that we submit ourselves to rulers only if under rules.[18]

Justice Douglas also pursued this interpretive strategy in his concurring opinion. He reasoned:

> The power of the Federal Government to condemn property is well established. It can condemn for any public purpose; and I have no doubt but that condemnation of a plant, factory, or industry in order to promote industrial peace would be constitutional. But there is a duty to pay for all property taken by the Government. The command of the Fifth Amendment is that no "private property be taken for public use, without just compensation." That constitutional requirement has an important bearing on the present case.
> The President has no power to raise revenues. That power is in the

Congress by Article I, Section 8 of the Constitution. The President
might seize and the Congress by subsequent action might ratify the
seizure. But until and unless Congress acted, no condemnation would
be lawful. The branch of government that has the power to pay compensation for a seizure is the only one able to authorize a seizure or
make lawful one that the President has effected.[19]

In short, the specificity of article I, section 8, coupled with the compensation obligation of the fifth amendment, eliminated any ambiguity in
the article II grants on the question of the President's power to seize
private property on his own authority.

If the text was ambiguous, the craftsmen would look, second, to the
original understanding to see if it shed any light on how broadly or narrowly the Court should construe the executive power and the general
grants of authority in article II. That the framers were concerned with
the scope of executive power is clear. They debated the question in the
Constitutional Convention,[20] and they debated it again during the
subsequent ratification debates.[21] While Hamilton admittedly favored a
strong executive, his views did not reflect the prevailing view among the
framers. Indeed, Hamilton privately dismissed the Constitution as a
"frail fabric" and expected the government that it established to fail
because it did not give the President sufficient authority.[22]

The historical milieu in which these debates and discussions occurred
might also illuminate the original understanding. The colonies had
rebelled against autocratic government. They despised King George and
his royal governors. As Justice Jackson drily reminded his brethren, the
framers had not fashioned the executive in the image of King George.[23]
Additionally, the state constitutions adopted after the Declaration of
Independence might demonstrate a general consensus about the
desirable scope of executive power.[24] Finally, the Court might have ex-
amined the philosophical works that influenced the thinking of the
framers.[25]

If an analysis of the original understanding on the point provided no
definitive answer, a court of craftsmen might look, third, to see if
historical practice provided one. President Truman was not the first
Chief Executive who exercised unspecified power to preserve domestic
welfare and national security. As early as 1793 President Washington
dispatched troops to quell the Whiskey Rebellion.[26] Even Jefferson, the
apostle of constitutinal restraint, purchased the Louisiana Territory
and fought an undeclared war with the Barbary pirates. The actions of

these Presidents would be especially pertinent since Washington was actively involved in the drafting and ratifying processes, and Jefferson contributed significantly to the intellectual debate among the Founders. Their actions would thus constitute a contemporary gloss on the original understanding.

On the more particularized question of whether the President could seize private property, the historical record was scarcely silent. Admittedly, none of the early Presidents seized private property. Indeed, as Justice Frankfurter pointed out: "Down to the World War II period...the record is barren of instances comparable to the one before us."[27] In his concurring opinion Justice Frankfurter nevertheless listed numerous incidents in this century in which modern Presidents had seized private property.[28] Justice Frankfurter thought almost all the seizures distinguishable from President Truman's seizure of the steel mills, primarily because in most instances the President purported to act pursuant to a congressional statute. The Justice explained: "In every case Congress has qualified this grant of power with limitations and safeguards. This body of enactments...demonstrates that Congress deemed seizure so drastic a power as to require that it be carefully circumscribed whenever the President was vested with this extraordinary authority."[29]

Assuming that the Constitution would permit Congress to authorize presidential seizure of private property, a court of craftsmen might check to see it any such statutes had been passed. In the *Steel Seizure* case the Justices in fact looked at several statutes which arguably authorized the President to seize private property.[30] The Chief Justice insisted that Congress had enacted numerous pieces of legislation whose successful implementation required a steady supply of steel. He reasoned that the Court should presume that Congress intended the President to take all necessary measures to implement those statutes. Although a court might tease such a purpose out of statutory language that did not explicitly state it, a court could not assert that a statute impliedly contemplated the President's use of a measure which Congress had specifically rejected as inappropriate. Here the Court found that Congress had decided that the President should not have broad power to seize private property. Justice Harold Burton (1945-1958) concluded his concurring opinion:

> The controlling fact here is that Congress, within its constitutionally delegated power, has prescribed for the President specific procedures,

exclusive of seizure, for his use in meeting the present type of emergency. Congress has reserved to itself the right to determine where and when to authorize the seizure of property in meeting such an emergency. Under these circumstances, the President's order of April 8 invaded the jurisdiction of Congress. It violated the essence of the principle of the separation of governmental powers. Accordingly, the injunction against its effectiveness should be sustained.[31]

Admittedly, none of the statutes explicitly authorized seizure. They would thus justify the seizure only if seizure was impliedly necessary to execute the policies embodied in them.

Thus, a craftsman could not escape an examination of public policy. Similarly, he must apply values. What distinguishes his approach from that of the statesman is that the public policies invoked are not his, but Congress's; the values invoked are not his, but the framers'. The craftsman does not choose those policies which commend themselves to his judgment. The craftsman accepts the policy judgments of Congress.[32] As Justice Frankfurter pointed out: "When Congress itself has struck the balance, has defined the weight to be given the competing interests, a court of equity is not justified in ignoring that pronouncement under the guise of exercising equitable discretion."[33] Here the Justice had no doubt about the policy choice Congress had made: it chose to deny the President the authority to seize production facilities as a remedy for any national emergency arising from a strike. Craftsmen do not apply those values which they prize. They respect those values which the framers prized. Thus, Justice Black closed his opinion for the Court with this stinging rebuke:

> The Founders of this Nation entrusted the lawmaking power to the Congress alone in both good and bad times. It would do no good to recall the historical events, the fears of power and the hopes for freedom that lay behind their choice. Such a review would but confirm our holding that this seizure order cannot stand.

In the *Steel Seizure* case the Court reached a craftsmen's result, although some Justices joined in that result for statesmen's reasons. The decision satisfied all the criteria of judicial craftsmanship. It was consistent with constitutional text, which did not authorize presidential seizure of private property. It was consistent with the original understanding, which was wary of broad executive power. It was consistent with underlying constitutional principles, particularly the separation of powers and checks and balances principles. The former principle suggested that Congress alone should exercise lawmaking authority; and, as Justice Black pointed out in his opinion for the Court, the President's seizure was essentially a lawmaking act.[35] The latter principle suggested that the Congress should exercise some check on the President; and, as the majority read the legislative history of the Taft-Hartley Act, Congress had told the President that he could not seize private property in order to settle a labor dispute. Finally, it was consistent with an unbroken record of historical practice, which suggested that a President could seize private property in an emergency only if he followed detailed procedures previously established by Congress. The President had admittedly ignored the two acts which did authorize seizure and had instead acted on his own. Thus the Court had to remind him that even he must obey the law.

In issuing that reminder, the Court reaffirmed the tenets of constitutionalism and supported the rule of law. Justice Jackson emphasized the importance of requiring the President to follow legal procedures even in emergencies:

> The essence of our free Government is "leave to live by no man's leave, underneath the law"—to be governed by those impersonal forces which we call law. Our Government is fashioned to fulfill this concept so far as humanly possible. The Executive, except for recommendation and veto, has no legislative power. The executive action we have here originates in the individual will of the President and represents an exercise of authority without law. No one, perhaps not even the President, knows the limits of the power he may seek to exert in this instance and the parties affected cannot learn the limit of their rights. We do not know today what powers over labor or property would be claimed to flow from Government possession if we should legalize it, what rights to compensation would be claimed or recognized, or on what contingency it would end. With all its defects, delays and inconveniences, men have discovered no technique for long preserving free government except that the Executive be under the law, and that the law be made by parliamentary deliberations.[36]

He then added a closing statement which stated succinctly the responsibility of the Court: "Such institutions may be destined to pass away. but it is the duty of the Court to be last, not first, to give them up."[37]

V. A Case Study in Contrasting Styles of Judicial Decision Making: How May Statesmen and Craftsmen Differ in Deciding Cases?

An analysis of the *Steel Seizure* case thus illuminates how differently statesmen and craftsmen would decide a question involving the scope of governmental power. The *Steel Seizure* case also illustrates how Justices may mix styles of judicial decision making. For example, judicial statesmen frequently employ a craftsmanlike style. Less frequently, judicial craftsmen will seek to enhance the persuasiveness of their decision by appealing to statesmanlike concerns. And more than occasionally, Justices will simply use both styles to justify the result. When Justices mix judicial decision making styles in this manner, they obscure the consequences of choosing one style rather than the other. An analysis of *Hawaii Housing Authority v. Midkiff*[1] will delineate more sharply the difference in consequences because in that case the Justices did not mix styles. Moreover, an analysis of the decision illustrates how differently statesmen and craftsmen would decide a case involving individual rights. In *Midkiff* the Court had to decide the meaning of the public use clause of the fifth amendment. That clause protects a property owner's rights by prohibiting the government from taking private property except for "public use." Specifically, the question was whether a state may take real property from a lessor and transfer title in fee simple absolute to a lessee because of a shortage of land available for fee simple residential ownership.[2]

This case arose out of an attempt by the Hawaii legislature to redistribute land. A small number of persons owned most of the privately held land in Hawaii, and they chose to lease their property rather than sell it. Seventy-two private landowners owned 47 percent of the land in Hawaii. Since the state and federal governments owned another 49 percent of the land, only 4 percent of the land was left for purchase by other private owners. On Oahu, Hawaii's most urbanized island, twenty-two private landowners owned 72.5 percent of the fee simple titles. The legislature decided that the practice of leasing rather than selling deprived too many people of the opportunity to own their own property and artificially inflated the cost of residential property. Consequently, the legislature enacted the Hawaii Land Reform Act.[3] Under the Act, the Hawaii Housing Authority (HHA) could transfer the property to present lessees if they met eligibility requirements. A tenant-lessee was eligible if he lived in a residential tract of at least five acres, owned a house in the tract, had a bona fide intent to live in the house or be a resident of the state, showed ability to purchase a fee interest in it, and did not own residential property nearby. The HHA could proceed only when twenty-five such tenant-lessees from the tract or eligible tenant-lessees from at least half the lots in the tract, whichever was less, applied to the HHA for transfer of title.

The Supreme Court upheld the Hawaii statute in an opinion that echoed statesmanship concerns. At least since *Euclid v. Amber Realty*[4] the Court's decisions have reflected the popular notion that modern government should regulate land use in the public interest. In these decisions the Court has consistently construed constitutional constraints on governmental authority narrowly and simultaneously construed the state's police powers broadly. In the specific context of takings cases, the Court had already determined that the power of eminent domain was but a particular police power and, perhaps more surprisingly, that the fifth amendment public use limitation on the state's exercise of its eminent domain power did not differ from the general due process limitation on the state's exercise of its police power.[5] Under this view, the government may take property, not only for public *use,* but also for any public *purpose.* In other words, the government need not show that it is taking the property for a public *use,* which presumably encompasses a narrower range of takings than would public purpose. Justice Douglas reminded his readers:

> The concept of the public welfare is broad and inclusive. The values it represents are spiritual as well as physical, aesthetic as well as monetary. It is within the power of the legislature to determine that the community should be beautiful as well as healthy, spacious as well as clean, well-balanced as well as carefully patrolled.... If those who govern the District of Columbia decide that the Nation's Capital should be beautiful as well as sanitary, there is nothing in the Fifth Amendment that stands in the way.[6]

Confident that public authorities would wisely exercise the powers thus conferred, the Court could and did adopt a deferential attitude toward legislative zoning decisions. Justices who usually scrutinized carefully any invasion of individual rights saw no reason to scrutinize carefully the state's claim that it was taking property for a public purpose. In a case in which a department store owner complained that his property was being taken for a nonpublic purpose, the Court dismissed his complaint as frivolous:

> ...when the legislature has spoken, the public interest has been declared in terms well-nigh conclusive. In such cases the legislature, not the judiciary, is the main guardian of the public needs to be served by social legislation.... [T]his principle admits of no exception merely because the power of eminent domain is involved. The role of the judiciary in determining whether that power is being exercised for a public purpose is an extremely narrow one.[7]

Indeed, Justice Sandra Day O'Connor (1981-   ) wrote as if the *Midkiff* decision was an a fortiori one from *Berman v. Parker:*

> There is, of course, a role for courts to play in reviewing a legislature's judgment of what constitutes a public use, even when the eminent domain power is equated with the police power. But the Court in *Berman* made clear that it is 'an extremely narrow' one.... [W]here the exercise of the eminent domain power is rationally related to a conceivable public purpose, the Court has never held a compensated taking to be proscribed by the Public Use Clause.
>
> On this basis, we have no trouble concluding that the Hawaii Act is constitutional. The people of Hawaii have attempted, much as the settlers of the original 13 Colonies did, to reduce the perceived social and economic evils of a land oligopoly traceable to their monarchs. The land oligopoly has, according to the Hawaii Legislature, created artificial deterrents to the normal functioning of the State's residential land market and forced thousands of individual homeowners to lease, rather than buy, the land underneath their homes. Regulating oligopoly and the evils associated with it is a classic exercise of a State's police powers. We cannot disapprove of Hawaii's exercise of this power.[8]

Perhaps the Justices shared the view that Hawaii, like third world countries, needed land reform if democratic institutions were to survive there.

The Court's decision and its rationale would have troubled a craftsman, who would have asked a number of questions. A craftsman would have asked why the Court characterized the taking as an exercise of the police power subject to no greater restrictions than those embodied in the due process clause. The craftsman would concede that the state usually justifies any taking as necessary to promote the public health, safety, and welfare—the traditional objects for which the state exercises its police powers. However, the fact that the state exercises its police and eminent domain powers for the same objectives does not necessarily mean that those powers are confined by the same limitations. Were that true, the craftsman might point out, there would have been no need to include the takings clause at all. Moveover, the statesman would have to admit that the power of eminent domain is subject to at least one limitation that does not confine the police power: the obligation to compensate. Consequently, the craftsman would conclude that the framers intended to restrict the state's exercise of its eminent domain powers more narrowly than its general police powers.

The craftsman would next ask if the framers intended to limit the state's exercise of its eminent domain powers only to the obligation to compensate the owner for the taking. On this point the language of the fifth amendment would be instructive, if not determinative. It reads: "nor shall private property be taken for public use, without just compensation." Apparently, the framers did not authorize any taking so long as it was compensated. They also insisted that the taking be for a public use. Indeed, public use rather than compensation would appear to be the major limitation intended by the framers. In short, the framers did distinguish between police powers generally and the particular power of eminent domain. They said to the government: when you exercise the power of eminent domain, you may take private property only for a public use and even then you must pay just compensation.[9]

Next, the craftsman would ask why the framers used "public use" rather than "public purpose." He would question whether the Court could simply assume that they meant public use to mean public purpose. Perhaps he would have recalled Justice Black's warning: "One of the most effective ways of diluting or expanding a constitutionally guaranteed right is to substitute for a crucial word or words of a constitutional guarantee another word or words, more or less flexible and more or less restricted in meaning."[10]

Consequently, the craftsman would question why the Court should permit this taking simply because the legislature has decided that land reform is desirable. Land reform may be desirable, of course. The craftsman would admit that he has no authority to decide that question. However, the Constitution does not permit the legislature to use any means it wishes to achieve its policy goals, however desirable they may be. Even the great Chief Justice Marshall, in the very decision in which he recognized that Congress had broad discretion in choosing the means by which to implement its policies, reminded Congress that it could not choose means expressly prohibited. The fifth amendment is just such a prohibition. It protects the rights of the private property owner. It guarantees him that the government will not take his property except for a public use.

Finally, the craftsman would point out that the Court cannot automatically defer to the legislative judgment that it is taking for a public use. However appropriate such deference might be were the question whether the taking was for a public purpose, it is inappropriate where the question is whether the taking violates a specific prohibition on its exercise. The Court should no more defer to a legislative judgment that the taking was for a public use than it should defer to a judgment that the compensation was just. To defer to the legislative judgment in such circumstances is to let the fox guard the hen-house.

In any case, one need not speculate on how a craftsman might have decided this case. One need only examine the opinion of Judge Alarcon, who wrote the Court of Appeals decision that the Supreme Court reversed.[11] In trying to define the scope of the public use limitation, Judge Alarcon looked to the language of the Constitution and to the intent of those who drafted it. The fifth amendment says that property may be taken only for "public use." Both words are critical. Presumably, the government may take for neither *private* use nor public *purpose*. The plain and ordinary meaning of "public use" is that the property taken will be open to the public. Condemnation for rights of way would thus be the paradigmatic taking for public use. Condemnation for the purpose of transferring the property from one private person to another private person for the latter's benefit would be the antiparadigmatic taking for public use.

To determine whether the framers intended public use to be given its plain and ordinary meaning, Judge Alarcon turned to the historical milieu in which the framers lived, to the debates at the Constitutional Convention, to arguments made during the ratification process, and to the statements of principals like Madison and Hamilton. From these sources Judge Alarcon concluded that the framers were "keenly mindful of the need to create a form of government which would protect each person's property interests."[12] Madison had confided his apprehensions to Jefferson:

> In our Governments the real power lies in the majority of the Community, and the invasion of private rights is *chiefly* to be apprehended, not from acts of Government contrary to the sense of its constituents, but from acts in which the Government is the mere instrument of the major number of Constituents.[13]

The framers looked with special horror on the forced redistribution of property.[14] Madison reminded his fellow delegates to the Constitutional Convention that property would never be safe in the hands of an unpropertied majority.[15] The Hawaii Land Reform Act would have confirmed Madison's worst fears. In light of this history one must characterize as astonishing Justice O'Connor's undocumented assertion that the people of Hawaii were only doing what the colonists had done two centuries before.

Judge Alarcon also looked to decisions immediately subsequent to the adoption of the Constitution. *Calder v. Bull*[16] was particularly instructive. In that case, Justice Chase declared that "a law that takes property from A and gives it to B is against all reason and justice." Since Chase's diagram would describe the facts of *Midkiff* as well as the facts of *Calder v. Bull*, one can safely conclude that the Justice would have struck down the Hawaii Land Reform Act.

Finally, Judge Alarcon surveyed historical practice. While he identified some instances in which courts had sustained nonparadigmatic takings, he also found general agreement on the one instance in which the government could not exercise the power of eminent domain: "The sovereign may not take the private property of A and transfer it to B solely for B's private use and benefit."[17] Of course, the Hawaii Land Reform Act violated this principle.

Moreover, Judge Alarcon decided that a court should "scrutinize carefully any legislative attempt to take private property" to insure that the attempt did not violate any constitutional provision. He read the public use clause as an express limitation on the government's power to take property. To read it otherwise "would be to ignore the explicit language of the Constitution and to disregard the fifth amendment protections granted to citizens of the states under the fourteenth amendment.''[18] The right to hold property free from condemnation for nonpublic use purposes is a fundamental right, and a court should protect it as zealously as it protects all other fundamental rights. Had the Supreme Court been as sensitive to its obligations as was Judge Alarcon, it would have affirmed his decision that the Hawaii Land Reform Act violated the public use limitation of the fifth and fourteenth amendments.

Such a decision would not necessarily have precluded Hawaii's achievement of land reform. Statesmen in the legislature could have chosen any number of other, presumably constitutional, means. The state could have sold off parts of its vast holdings, for example. It might have persuaded the national government to do likewise. Still another choice would have been to make present landowners the proverbial offer they could not refuse. In other words, the state itself could have anted up a price sufficient to induce present owners to sell, and it then could have resold the land.

VI. The Case For Craftsmanship: Why Should Justices Decide as Craftsmen?

Critics of craftsmanship dismiss it as a viable method of judging for two reasons. First, they insist that men cannot divorce themselves from their biases and prejudices. Consequently, they scoff at the prospect of a detached judge objectively searching for "the law."[1] Second, they insist the constitutional text is ambiguous and the historical record is either so sparse or so contradictory that it cannot illuminate that ambiguity.[2] Specifically, critics insist either that the framers had no collective intentions[3] or that their intentions cannot be recreated.[4] Alternatively, other critics argue that the only discoverable intentions will be so general as to provide no guidance for decision.[5] Consequently, critics deride the assertion that the original understanding requires a particular result. These are powerful criticisms; and, if true, they eviscerate the case for craftmanship.

Examples drawn from history, however, prove that Justices can transcend their biases and prejudices. Justice James McReynolds (1914-1941) hated Germans so intensely that he publicly urged a group of young men "to kill Huns and to keep killing Huns."[6] Yet he rebuked a state legislature animated by the same hate for forbidding the teaching of German.[7] The Justice concluded that "the law"—the Constitution— guaranteed a person the right to study any language he wished. Justice Brandeis had little confidence in most New Deal legislation.[8] Yet he repeatedly voted to sustain that legislation.[9] The Justice concluded that "the law"—the Constitution—permitted Congress to enact legislation that he thought harebrained.

Modern psychology also confirms what history teaches.[10] While some persons cannot escape their biases and prejudices, others can. Detachment and objectivity are recognized mental faculties. Persons who possess these faculties can decide "correctly" on the basis of identified criteria even though they may disagree with the criteria or disapprove the particular result.

The ideal judge thus has a particular psychological makeup rather than a particular set of values. The political, economic, and social profile of the ideal judge is as varied as humankind. He may come from the ghetto or a country estate. He may have worked his way through state universities or attended posh private schools. He may have pushed radical causes zealously, hewed to traditional views quietly, or held himself aloof from political battles. Ideal judges share one and only one common quality: they are detached and objective.[11] What sets them apart from their less than ideal brethren is their ability to detach themselves from their personal views and decide the case before them objectively on the basis of the law.

In constitutional cases, that law must include the text and its original understanding. Neither is as ambiguous or as unilluminating as critics of craftsmanship allege. In the first place, all constitutional cases ultimately raise claims about the nature of man, the role of government, and the appropriate relationship between man and government; and the men who framed the Constitution had definite views on all three kinds of claims. Moreover, the fundamental problem of reconciling governmental power with respect for individual liberty has not changed since 1789. Consequently, the principles and values embodied in the Constitution provide a basis for the reasoned elaboration of its text and its application to a particular contemporary problem. In effect they become the major premise in a syllogistic argument that the particular problem is within or without the constitutional rule.[12]

A common experience confirms that knowledge of a person's general values can tell one how to solve a problem consistent with the person's values—even though the person has expressed no specific intention about how the problem should be resolved. Fiduciaries and agents, though they may occasionally feel the need to consult their principals for clarification, regularly act without such consultation. The law presumes that they can execute their principal's wishes. Justice Rehnquist graphically underscored the common sense of the matter in *Carey v. Population Services International*.[13] Dissenting from the Court's decision that the Constitution conferred on minors a fundamental right of access to contraceptives, the Justice tartly observed:

> If those responsible for [the Bill of Rights and the Civil War] Amendments...could have lived to know that their efforts had enshrined in

the Constitution the right of commercial vendors of contraceptives to peddle them to unmarried minors through such means as window displays and vending machines located in the men's room of truck stops, notwithstanding the considered judgment of the New York Legislature to the contrary, it is not difficult to imagine their reaction.[14]

Consider, for example, the claim that compelled participation in a lineup violates the fifth amendment privilege against self-incrimination. Admittedly, the bare text does not provide any definitive answer to the claim. So far as one can tell from the text itself, it might only prohibit the police from beating confessions out of a suspect. Alternatively, it might prohibit requiring the suspect to give any information or do anything that might provide evidence against him. Under the former definition, the particular claim would be excluded. Under the latter definition, the particular claim would be included.

The guarantee against compelled incrimination, however, grew out of a particular history that illuminates the bare text. Professor Leonard Levy, in his book on the origins of the privilege against self-incrimination, points out that the privilege is in fact a right rooted in early English history.[15] Specifically, the right against self-incrimination emerged from the struggle to establish an accusatorial system as a check on governmental power. Justice Abe Fortas (1965-1969) summarized the import of that historic struggle:

> A man may be punished, even put to death, by the state; but...he should not be made to prostrate himself before its majesty. *Mea culpa* belongs to a man and his God. It is a plea that cannot be exacted from free men by human authority. To require it is to insist that the state is the superior of the individuals who compose it, instead of their servants.[16]

Unfortunately, much of that history has been largely forgotten. Were that history remembered, the right would be seen as a broad libertarian principle that a person may not be compelled to speak against himself.

Professor Levy explains:

> The framers of the Bill of Rights saw their injunction, that no man should be a witness against himself in a criminal case, as a central feature of the accusatory system of criminal justice. While deeply committed to perpetuating a system that minimized the possibilities of convicting the innocent, they were not less concerned about the humanity

that the fundamental law should show even to the offender. Above all, the Fifth Amendment reflected their judgment that in a free society, based on respect for the individual, the determination of guilt or innocence by just procedures, in which the accused made no unwilling contribution to his conviction, was more important than punishing the guilty.[17]

Unfortunately, the Court's interpretations of the self-incrimination clause have not always been faithful to the principle embodied in it.[18] This example nevertheless illustrates that the diligent judge can discover the views of the framers through an examination of the text and its history. Moreover, a court that makes clear its determination to rely on the original understanding will elicit briefing and oral argument on the subject. Consequently, the judge need not be a historian. He need not bury himself in the bowels of the Library of Congress. He himself will not likely sift through musty letters or gently handle crumbling newspapers from the eighteenth century. Rather, he will rely, as judges always have relied, on the resourceful and thorough presentations of the lawyers who appear before him. The lawyer will in turn rely, as lawyers always have relied, on experts, whose knowledge and work the lawyer assimilates, summarizes, and communicates.

So far from being sparse, the materials relevant to the original understanding are voluminous. The founding period is well-chronicled. We know what and whom the framers read. We know the conflicts that shaped their constitutional views, and we know the lessons that they drew from those conflicts. They wrote and spoke about them, and we know what they said. We know how they translated these lessons into the first state constitutions. We have detailed records of the Constitutional Convention itself and of the subsequent state ratification debates. We can consult the debates in the early Congresses, which were filled with those who had participated in the Convention and the public debate that followed it. We can examine the policies of the early Presidents. Washington chaired the Constitutional Convention. Adams was the "Atlas of American Independence." Jefferson articulated the values of the founding generation in the Declaration of Independence. Madison fathered the Constitution. A list of the men who served in their administrations reads like a Who's Who of the founding period.[19] These sources all illuminate the text.

Voluminous as are the materials on the original understanding, they admittedly do not always yield a clear, specific answer to the particular question being asked. Nor do they always yield a value or a principle of sufficient specificity to guide the craftsman's judgment. Consider, for example, the due process clause. Since the due process clause does not itself specify the process which is due, the Court must determine in every case what process is due. The judge can and should ask why the framers demanded due process, and the answer may give him standards by which he can eliminate some particular procedures. The standards are likely to be of such generality, however, that a range of other procedures will survive the "standard" cut and yet arguably not be necessary for the protection of life, liberty, or property in the particular case. Unless the judge is therefore prepared to say that due process is either a fixed set of procedures or those particular sets of procedures used in different classes of cases in 1791 (or, in the case of the fourteenth amendment, 1868), he cannot escape the responsibility for identifying the procedures required by due process on some basis other than the original understanding.

In those circumstances the best test of whether a particular procedure is constitutionally necessary or unnecessary is historical practice. The judge who relies on historical practice as a supplementary guide to application of the Constitution exercises no independent discretion; rather, he effectuates the purpose of the framers. As Marshall said, the framers wrote a constitution for ages to come and expected it to be adapted to the various crises of mankind.[20] He did not mean that the framers expected the Court to rewrite the Constitution periodically as they deemed necessary. He meant instead that the Constitution gave the people, speaking through their representatives, broad latitude to devise new solutions to old problems or novel solutions to unanticipated problems.

Thus, the Court should treat those general constitutional clauses like the due process clause as a skeletal framework. Historical practice is the flesh that the people have put on the constitutional skeleton. The Court should therefore look to historical practice when the original understanding provides no clear, specific answer. In that way the Court does insure that the Constitution remains a living document because it allows the people, through their practices, to give substantive content to its general clauses. Moreover, the Court in this way defers to the sovereign authority of the people ultimately to interpret their Constitution.

The right-to-counsel problem is illustrative. Outside the criminal trial context,[21] a person's right to the assistance of counsel is a question of due process. The present Court now decides whether due process guarantees an indigent the assistance of appointed counsel on the basis of a three-pronged test. The test requires the Justices to balance three competing considerations: the nature and magnitude of the individual interest at stake, the government's interest in economy and efficiency, and the probability that particular procedures will reduce the likelihood of an erroneous decision.[22] In *Eldridge v. Mathews,* the case in which the Court first enunciated this test, it made no effort to demonstrate that these particular factors were the ones that, historically or traditionally, the community had used in deciding what process was due. Neither did the Court inquire what was the common practice elsewhere (i.e., in other jurisdictions) in proceedings of the kind before it. Instead, the Court manufactured the test from its own prior declarations. It bluntly said: "[O]ur prior decisions indicate that identification of the specific dictates of due process generally requires consideration of three distinct factors...."[23] The Court thus elevated what it had said over what the Constitution and the people had said.[24]

The Court's balancing test is unrooted in historical tradition and insensitive to current practice. It does not reflect what communities used to do about providing counsel for indigents; neither does it reflect what communities presently do about providing counsel for indigents. Consequently, the rule does not embody either present or past wisdom about the need for counsel, the costs of providing it, and the relative benefits of providing it rather than other social benefits. Justice Rehnquist has correctly observed that "[i]t is impossible to build sound constitutional doctrine upon a mistaken understanding of constitutional history."[25]

Moreover, the rule gives the Justices a largely untrammeled discretion to grant whatever process five of them deem desirable or reasonable or just. Like legislators, they are thus free to fashion public policy, and they do. The modern Court regularly invokes multifactor tests in many other areas, and the Justices manipulate them to justify the Court's imposition of whatever privately preferred public policy commends itself to five or more of them.

These multifactor tests are so vacuous that they can justify conflicting public policies; and the Court often splits, each side vehemently defending its balancing of the factors as correct. The Court's decision in *Lassiter v. Department of Social Services*[26] is illustrative. In that case the Court had to decide whether an indigent parent was entitled to the services of appointed counsel at a hearing to terminate her parental rights. All nine Justices agreed to decide the case on the basis of the three-pronged *Eldridge* test. The Justices split 5-4, however, on the result. The majority rejected the claim, a legitimate decision if it could discern no common practice in the area. Justice Potter Stewart (1958-1981), however, appeared to justify the decision on public policy grounds, the most important of which was the wisdom of the Court's deferring to the factual determinations of the trial judge. The dissenters, animated by notions of equality, would have sustained the claim.

Of course, craftsmen also may disagree among themselves. That is scarcely surprising. The inquiry into the original understanding is itself a difficult one, and the extrapolation and application of the framers' values and insights to a particular problem beyond their contemplation is extraordinarily difficult. Moreover, reasonable persons may disagree about the nature and extent of historical practice. In such circumstances uniform and unanimous conclusions even among craftsmen are not to be expected. What can be expected is a substantially increased likelihood that craftsmen will get the right answers because they are asking the right questions. There is, after all, little hope that the Court will ever get the right answers unless it asks the right questions. What did the framers intend? What were their values? Upon what principles did they act?

Moreover, the craftsman's focus on the original understanding will narrow the scope of disagreement even where it does not yield uniform and clear conclusions. An example from contemporary constitutional litigation will illustrate this point. Cases involving alleged racial discrimination have vexed the Court for many years. Whether the equal protection clause of the fourteenth amendment was intended to prohibit segregated schools may be unclear.[27] Whether its framers contemplated that federal judges would exercise broad remedial powers to eliminate the effects of de jure segregation may be debated.[28] What may not be debated is its framers' antipathy to any legislation that intentionally disfavored an identified race because of its race.[29]

Admittedly, many of those who framed the Constitution itself were racists. The Constitution recognized slavery, and the Bill of Rights did not include an equal protection guarantee. But those who framed the Constitution allowed for its amendment. After the Civil War the people exercised that right and abolished slavery and guaranteed all persons the equal protection of the laws. Although many who favored the fourteenth amendment were also racists, they adamantly insisted that public authorities treat all races equally. They therefore would not countenance an official conferring or denying a public benefit or burden on the basis of the person's race.

In light of that history, at least one class of racial discrimination cases ought not to trouble the Court. Affirmative action intentionally favors blacks and disfavors whites because of their respective races. Examine the cases that the Court has decided. A state-funded medical school set aside a number of seats in its entering class for minorities, considered minority applicants in a separate admissions process, and admitted minority applicants with lower indicators than rejected white applicants presented.[30] A company agreed to select a fixed number of black employees for training programs even though they did not satisfy eligibility criteria as clearly as did some rejected whites.[31] Congress insisted that contractors give a fixed percentage of their business to minority owned enterprises.[32] Caught in a budget crunch, a local city laid off more senior white firemen because it would otherwise undermine the "advances" achieved through its earlier preferential hiring program for minorities.[33] Justice Harry Blackmun (1970-   ) gave this "Truthspeak" explanation for these programs, all of which he found constitutionally permissible: "[T]o get beyond race, we must take account of race."[34]

"Taking race into account" was, however, precisely what the framers of the fourteenth amendment wanted to prohibit. They envisioned a society in which all persons would enjoy equal opportunities before the law and receive equal treatment from the law, regardless of race.[35] Consequently, affirmative action mandated by government is unconstitutional because it requires preferential treatment because of race. The equal protection clause forbids it, and a Court of craftsmen would enforce that prohibition.

Craftsmanship is thus a viable method of judging, and an analysis of the cases involving government aid to religious schools will confirm that conclusion. The school aid cases all raise the same general question: to what extent, if at all, may the government support religious schools? The Constitution addresses that question most directly and specifically in the first clause of the first amendment: "Congress shall make no law respecting an establishment of religion...."

The present Court does not analyze school aid cases in light of the framers' understanding of that clause, but instead uses a three-pronged test purportedly derived from the framers' understanding but fashioned in fact out of the Justices' pragmatic concerns as statesmen.[36] Under this test a state many aid religious schools only if (1) its primary purpose is secular; (2) the primary effect of the aid neither advances nor inhibits religion; and (3) the aid will not lead to excessive entanglement between church and state.

However helpful these three considerations may be as a guide to legislative decision making, they are not the factors which prompted the framers—that is, the first Congress, which proposed the first amendment—to adopt the antiestablishment clause. Two principal concerns emerged in the congressional debate over what became the first amendment.[37] First, Congress sought to preserve state autonomy over establishment questions. At that time several states had established churches. Congress did not want the national government to have the power to disestablish those churches. It wanted instead to insure that the states remained free to make their own decisions about establishments. Even Professor William Winslow Crosskey, who is almost alone in arguing that Congress intended the Bill of Rights to apply against both the national and state governments, agrees that Congress intended the antiestablishment clause to apply only against the national government.[38] Indeed, the fact that the explicit textual injunction which precedes the clause—"Congress shall make no law..."—is not thereafter repeated is the chief textual argument in Crosskey's case that, conversely, Congress did intend the other provisions to apply against the states.

Congress wanted, second, to prohibit the establishment of a national church. That concern is both consistent with and necessary to preservation of state autonomy over establishment questions.[39] Indeed, the absolute prohibition on congressional authority to make any law respecting an establishment of religion makes perfect sense if establishment of religion is understood to include any state establishments which then existed or might thereafter come into existence. If Congress could establish a national church, it could supplant the then-existing state establishments. The framers therefore had no choice but to prohibit the establishment of a national church and deny Congress any authority over state establishments. The language which they carefully chose did just that.

Thus, the first Congress intended only to deny Congress the power to establish a national church or to disestablish state churches. Specifically, the framers did not intend to prohibit Congress from enacting legislation that might favor religious enterprises.[40] Congress was not animated by any hostility to religion. No anticlerical principle explains the establishment clause. No anticlerical values explain the establishment clause. On the contrary, the framers believed that individual virtue was essential to the success of a self-governing republic, and they thought that churches inculcated that virtue in citizens of the republic.[41] In light of those beliefs, the framers intended only to prohibit Congress from favoring a particular religion. Thus, they left Congress free to aid religious enterprises generally if it thought that wise.

This congressional understanding of the establishment clause would require craftsmen to decide contemporary government-aid-to-religion cases very differently from the way in which the Court now decides them. In the first place, the Court would have to distinguish between state aid programs and national aid programs, because the framers clearly envisioned that state governments would retain far broader powers to legislate in favor of religious enterprises than would Congress.[42] In light of the framers' tolerance of state establishments, a Court of craftsmen could not strike any state aid programs on establishment grounds. Particular state programs might violate other constitutional strictures, of course;[43] but they would not be unconstitutional simply because they advanced religion and involved the state in religion. Since state establishments did both, the framers must have intended to preserve a state's preexisting power to establish a church and to protect such establishments from any hostile national legislation. A Congress that denied itself and its successors the power to interfere with state establishments could hardly have contemplated that the Court could exercise such power.

Those who recoil in horror at the prospect that a state might establish a church should remember that the Constitution would only permit it, not command it. Those states that had established churches had abolished them by 1850.[44] The states abolished their establishments because the people demanded their abolition, not because the Court ordered their abolition. In short, the political process worked. The people decided as a matter of public policy that they did not want established churches. They did not go to the Court and ask the Justices to decree that policy because it was wise and just. Rather, they convinced their fellow citizens that the state should not maintain an established church, and then they persuaded the legislature to act on that consensus. Or perhaps they insisted on a state constitutional prohibition against any establishment of religion.

National aid programs would pose more troublesome questions for craftsmen, for the framers gave Congress no carte blanche in religious matters. Still, the relatively narrow scope of the prohibition on congressional authority would provide considerable guidance. Congress could not enact two kinds of laws. First, it could not enact laws that touched state establishments. Since there are no state establishments today, Congress would not likely run afoul of that prohibition.

Second, Congress could not enact laws that established or, perhaps, tended to establish a religion. In cases raising such questions the Court would have to define "establishment of religion" and perhaps identify the steps that tended toward such establishments. The latter step in particular might prove troublesome, and application of either set of criteria to a given set of facts might be difficult.

Still, Congress would not likely run afoul of this prohibition because neutral legislation that did not prefer any particular religion would pass muster under the establishment clause, construed as the framers understood it. Most commonly, government seeks to defray the cost of private education, much of which is provided by church related schools. For example, it pays for transportation, textbooks, testing, and tutoring. As long as the government offers these benefits to all, it would not violate the establishment clause. So long as construction grants, salary supplements, and tuition tax credits were similarly extended to all, they too would pass constitutional muster because the core requirement of the establishment clause is that Congress treat all religions evenhandedly.[45]

The effect of this understanding would be to remit to the political process most questions about whether and to what extent the government should aid religion. That result is scarcely surprising in view of the framers' general preference for legislative resolution of public policy questions. What must be understood is that the question is one of public policy rather than one involving the fundamental liberties of the people. Free exercise, not freedom from establishment, is the fundamental religious right protected by the first amendment. As Justice Black observed in *Engel v. Vitale:* "The Establishment Clause, unlike the Free Exercise Clause, does not depend on any showing of direct governmental compulsion and is violated by the enactment of laws which establish an official religion whether those laws operate directly to coerce non-observing individuals or not."[46]

The mere fact that a taxpaying citizen may have to support religious enterprises in which he does not believe does not offend the Constitution any more than the Constitution is offended whenever the government spends funds to support programs to which the taxpaying citizen has religious objections.[47] One who has religious objections to capital punishment cannot refuse to pay that proportion of his taxes used to fund executions. One who has religious objections to abortions cannot refuse to pay that proportion of taxes used to fund abortions. However strong the moral and philosophical objections to such compulsion, they do not generally make such compulsion unconstitutional.

Precisely because the moral and philosophical objections to such compulsion are so strong, debate over government aid programs may be bitter and divisive. Consequently, some Justices insist that the Court should prohibit legislatures and Congress from enacting laws that might generate political division along religious lines.[48] Quite aside from the difficulty of the Court's assessing such a problematic potential, the suggestion is a curious one. In a democratic republic, bitter division is commonplace, and sometimes these divisions are generated by differences of religious opinion. The framers believed that such bitter division should be channeled into legislative debate from which healing solutions might emerge. The general question of whether and to what extent the government should aid religious schools does not differ from other divisive questions like whether and to what extent the government should finance abortion, engage in deficit financing, or aid foreign rebels. These are precisely the kinds of questions which the people, not the Court, must answer.

The craftsman thus approaches the interpretive task with a clear goal in mind and a clear procedure for achieving that goal. His goal is to implement the intentions or purposes of the framers. He accomplishes that goal by looking, first, to the text and then, second, to the original understanding. Only if those fail to provide dispositive evidence of the framers' will does he look, third, to historical practice.

VII. The Case Against Statesmanship: Why Should Justices Refrain from Deciding as Statesmen?

Statesmanship as a method of judging is celebrated for several reasons. One of the most common is that it frees society from the dead hand of the past. Why, ask statesmen, should we be prohibited from doing something desirable just because some men who died two hundred years ago thought it was unwise? The plaintive question has a certain rhetorical appeal—until one remembers that the Constitution permits far more than it prohibits. Among its many "permits," it permits the present generation to abolish any current constitutional prohibitions through amendment.

Unless the framers intended the amendment process to be nothing more than an alternative to judicial amendment through statesmanlike reinterpretation of the Constitution, the Court itself cannot revise the Constitution. Indeed, judges who decide cases as statesmen usurp lawmaking authority from the people and thus undermine the rule of law. They sap the normal law-creation process by which the people and their representatives thrash out the rules that govern the society. More specifically, a Court of statesmen encourages an often all-too-willing Congress to abdicate its responsibility to decide what the law ought to be and whether that law is constitutional.[1] When Congress debated the Equal Rights Amendment, for example, its supporters repeatedly responded to questions about its meaning with "that's an issue for the courts to decide." An exasperated Senator finally exploded: "I think we ought to determine some of these things in the Congress of the United States, because we are elected to determine them, not unelected judges who are not....[T]he courts determine unanticipated conflicts. That is the purpose of the courts. But we are discussing fully anticipated conflicts."[2] Judge Malcolm Wilkey despairs: "The instances in which congressional legislation is deliberately left to the courts could be listed endlessly. The Congress' solution for all difficult drafting or decision-making dilemmas, 'leave it to the courts,' has become instinctive, habitual, chronic, and endemic.''[3] Congress now routinely follows the advice Franklin Roosevelt first gave them: it leaves any doubts about the constitutionality of the laws it passes to the courts.[4] Congressmen seem to have forgotten that they have an independent obligation to determine the constitutionality of the laws they pass.[5] In such circumstances the courts might be forgiven if they ignored the traditional presumption that legislation is constitutional, a presumption consistent with judicial respect for the popular lawmaking processes. Unfortunately, the Supreme Court has aided and abetted this congressional abdication.

Finally, the Court may defuse popular pressure for law reform by rushing into what it perceives to be a breach. Justice Frankfurter once reminded his fellow Justices:

> The framers carefully and with deliberate forethought refused so to enthrone the judiciary. In this situation, as in others of like nature, appeal for relief does not belong here. Appeal must be to an informed and civilly militant electorate. In a democratic society like ours, relief must come through an aroused popular conscience that sears the conscience of the people's representatives.[6]

In a democracy, popular pressure rather than judicial edicts should induce legislative action.

Defenders of judicial statesmanship are sensitive to the charge that it is antidemocratic. Some try to explain that the values invoked by judicial statesmen are in fact rooted in the Constitution. Others argue that the people share the values invoked by judicial statesmen. Perhaps the most astonishing answer to the charge that "noninterpretive review" is inconsistent with representative democracy is Professor Michael Perry's. He argues that such concern is misplaced because Congress, which is representative of the people, may discipline the Court.[7] In the first place, the answer implicitly concedes that a Court of statesmen is just another political actor,[8] a perception which would—if widely shared—compromise the moral authority of the Court.[9] In the second place, the professor exaggerates the effectiveness of such political controls, which Congress has seldom invoked successfully. One reason may be that Congress must overcome the force of political inertia, which in a democracy ought not to favor nonrepresentative institutions. The forces of inertia reinforce any Court decision, of course; but that result is unobjectionable if the Court is merely executing the wishes of the people as embodied in their Constitution. Where, contrariwise, the Court imposes its statesman's will, it thumbs its nose at representative institutions.

The blunt truth is that judicial statesmen do not have confidence in representative bodies.[10] Professor Perry asserts:

> As a matter of comparative institutional competence, the politically insulated federal judiciary is more likely when the human rights issue is a deeply controversial one, to move us in the direction of a right answer (assuming there is such a thing) than is the political process left to its own devices, which tends to resolve such issues by reflective mechanical reference to established moral conventions.[11]

Because Professor Perry rejects the claims of history, he may perhaps be forgiven the naivete of the assertion.[12] The Court never declared the Alien and Sedition Acts unconstitutional.[13] Rather, the President freed those held and remitted their fines.[14] The Court declared that black men had no rights which white men need respect.[15] The Congress and the states added the thirteenth, fourteenth, and fifteenth amendments to insure racial equality. The Court approved the forced internment of American citizens. The Congress later paid reparations to those interned.

Judicial statesmen are also celebrated for their ability to articulate the broad ethical principles which should guide us in our decision making. However, the judicial statesman may also act whimsically or capriciously because he must necessarily focus on the particular case before him. This particularized focus may distort the judgment of one who believes that he must do justice rather than simply determine whether the particular case falls within or without a general class. More often than not, in fact, a Court of statesmen must decide such cases on an ad hoc basis much as a legislature, uncommitted to principle and unbound by its prior decisions, may consider afresh any recurrent question of public policy. Consequently, the Court's decisions have become what Justice Roberts feared: a one-way train ticket good for this day and train only.[16]

Consider, for example, the Court's flip-flop in the *National League of Cities* series of cases. In *National League of Cities v. Usery*[17] the Court said that Congress could not force cities and states to pay their employees minimum wages. The four-person plurality opinion, written by Justice Rehnquist, reflected a principled commitment to federalism. Justice Rehnquist insisted that the states retained control over sovereign functions, and he reasoned that compliance with the national minimum wage standards would impede the state's discharge of those sovereign functions. Justice Blackmun provided the necessary fifth vote in a Hamlet-like concurrence. He said, first, that the dissents had made a lot of good points but that, second, he did not think the plurality's principle was as broad as the dissenters feared and that, anyway, on the specific facts of the case he agreed with the balance struck by the plurality.

In a series of subsequent cases, the Court waffled on the application of *National League of Cities*.[18] Not surprisingly, the Court began the process by distilling a multifactor test out of the *National League of Cities* case. Such tests are invariably fact-dependent, and the *National League of Cities* dissenters, joined by Justice Blackmun, found increasingly refined factual bases for distinguishing *National League of Cities*. Repeatedly, they upheld congressional power over local and state governments. Finally, the new Court majority decided to admit the obvious: it did not like the *National League of Cities* principle. In *Garcia v. San Antonio Metropolitan Transit Authority*[19] the Court overruled *National League of Cities*. Speaking through Justice Blackmun, the Court declared: "We doubt that courts ultimately can identify principled constitutional limitations on the scope of Congress' Commerce Clause powers over the State merely by relying on a prior definition of state sovereignty."[20]

Justice Rehnquist wrote the most interesting dissent, at least with respect to the point being discussed. The Justice did not repeat a principled defense of the original decision, as did his fellow dissenters Justices Lewis Powell (1972-   ) and O'Connor. Instead, he bluntly warned the majority: "I do not think it incumbent on those of us in dissent to spell out further the fine points of a principle that will, I am confident, in time again command the support of a majority of this Court."[21] Seldom if ever has a Justice so clearly mimicked the political branches in reminding the present majority that a newly "elected" majority can overturn the policy of a present majority.

The Court's retreat from principled decision making to "ad hocery" in these areas illustrates another undesirable characteristic of judicial statesmenship. It tends to produce divided courts whose decisions give little or no guidance to the community. The late, distinguished scholar Henry Hart criticized the Warren Court on that very ground:

> Only opinions which are grounded in reason and not on mere fiat or precedent can do the job which the Supreme Court of the United States has to do. Only opinions of this kind can be worked with by other men who have to take a judgment rendered on one set of facts and decide how it should be applied to a cognate but still different set of facts.[22]

This unfortunate result is not surprising. However difficult it may be to divine the original understanding and analyze a contemporary problem in its light, reconciling competing equities is far more difficult. Yet that is precisely what statesmen must do, and often each Justice has a particular variant of the general solution that in his view more sensitively resolves the problem. The geometric increase in concurring opinions in recent decades probably reflects this phenomenon. As a result, the Court increasingly disposes of cases through coalitions held together solely by a common agreement on the result. Again, the Court mimics the legislature, where result-oriented coalitions are common. Unfortunately, the Court must perform functions not given the legislature, and these coalition dispositions affect the performance of many of those functions.

One of those functions is to clarify the law. So long as judicial statesmen insist on concealing the general grounds for their decisions or persist in issuing ad hoc decrees, they cannot fulfill this function. One difficulty with their charade is that it misleads the uninitiated or unsuspecting. Unaware that the statesman delivers his opinion with a wink and a knowing smile, the uninitiated and unsuspecting mistake form for substance. They rely on the articulated rationale. That rationale may inform all their future plans, but it is not the real rationale for the decision. Anyone who relies on it does so at his own risk.

Some apologists for statesmanship have tried to turn this argument on its head. Professor Brest claims that reliance on the original understanding "produces a highly unstable constitutional order. The claims of scholars like William Winslow Crosskey and Raoul Berger demonstrate that a settled constitutional understanding is in perpetual jeopardy of being overturned by new light on the adopters' intent— shed by the discovery of historical documents, reexaminations of known documents, and reinterpretations of political and social history.''[23] Historical revisionism is of course a fact of life, and craftsmen must concede that constitutional questions are never rightly settled until they are settled in conformity with the original understanding. Still, the whole life of any historical view seems considerably longer than the whole life of a typical judicial statesman's commitment to a particular ground of decision.[24]

Moreover, the judicial statesman conceals the rationale of his opinion, and he thereby deprives it of the clarity that those who plan for the future need. Even the sophisticated can only guess about the real rationale, for craft requirements prevent the statesman from announcing his real rationale. Thus, the statesman who prides himself on deciding wisely for the future often cannot provide clear guidance to those who would build that future.

Most contemporary critics who urge the Justices to act as statesmen do not, in fact, urge the Court to decide cases in an unprincipled way or to conceal their grounds of decision.[25] To the contrary, they often entreat the Court to follow some particular principle or value.[26] These commentators have served the Justices a staggeringly rich and varied buffet of metaprinciples and values from which to choose: the principle of equal citizenship;[27] an antidiscrimination principle;[28] the principle of representative reinforcement[29]—to mention but a few.

These principles and values share one common denominator. None is demonstrably rooted in the text of the Constitution or in the original understanding.[30] Indeed, each is substituted for the text and its original understanding. Professor Owen Fiss explains:

> This...mode of constitutional interpretation deemphasizes the text. Primary reliance is instead placed on a set of principles—which I call mediating because they "stand between" the courts and the Constitution—to give meaning and content to an ideal embodied in the text. These principles are offered as a paraphrase of the particular textual provision, but in truth the relationship is much more fundamental. They give the provision its only meaning as a guide for decision. So much so, that over time one often loses sight of the artificial status of these principles—they are not "part of" the Constitution, but instead only a judicial gloss, open to reevaluation and redefinition in a way that the text of the Constitution is not.[31]

Professor Fiss concedes that these principles are exceedingly general. From his point of view their very generality is what makes them useful.

The "heroic" judge will "exploit" their generality to promote moral justice.[32]

> The judicial function will usually be one of working out the implica-
> tions of broad, imprecise moral ideals or principles. And in applying
> an ideal or principle as a decisional norm in a particular case, the
> Court necessarily redefines the ideal with greater precision by specify-
> ing the ideal's "content." Thus, the Court does not play a passive role
> in determining societal morality but an active, even creative one: the
> Court gives shape to that morality.[32]

What is surprising in all this is that these very commentators, who
laughingly pooh-poohed as naive and unsophisticated the idea that
general principles or values abstracted out of the text of the Constitution or its original understanding could guide judicial decision making,
insist that the statesmen judges who apply their principles or values will
be led inexorably to the right decision. The Court's failure to spell out a
privacy principle that logically dictates results in particular cases
disproves the claim, however.[33] Precisely because these principles or
values are unrooted in a historical context from which meaning may be
gleaned, they remain empty abstractions into which the judicial
statesman may pour any content he wishes.

Whether nine life-tenured judges are the ones to decide what the content of our fundamental law should be is doubtful. First, the Court is so
small, so insulated, and so narrow in its knowledge, expertise, and experience that it cannot effectively decide broad questions of public
policy. Because it is not representative of the many interest groups that
have a stake in the outcome, it may ignore or overlook valuable points
of view. Indeed, the Court is the most waspish institution in the government. Because the typical Justice is old, male, well-educated, and well-
off, the Justices will not likely derive any collective inspiration or insight from their varied experiences or their diverse roots in the community.[34] Yet enduring public policy must take into account the moral
sensibilities of the whole society.

Some commentators have sought to alleviate this concern by pointing
out that no single Justice can impose his idiosyncratic view. Professor
Robert Sedler reassures us:

> The point, then, is that different Justices may look to different sources
> to determine what values should be infused into the broadly phrased

and open-ended provisions of the Constitution. Although a Justice's personal values may conceivably influence that Justice's opinion of what values should be infused into a provision, what emerges in constitutional adjudication is an institutional decision of the Court. It is the institutional value infusion of the Court rather than the personal values of the individual Justices that ultimately controls.[35]

When one recalls that a camel is a horse designed by a committee, one must have considerable reservations about the desirability of any principle fashioned by a committee.

Second, the Court's procedures preclude its acting effectively as a deliberative body on questions of public policy. It lacks the staff to inform itself; and counsel, who can speak for only thirty minutes, cannot perform that function either. Even amicus briefs and the "Brandeis brief" do not provide the Court with the breadth and depth of information needed for public policy making. Moreover, the Court decides in secret. It cannot submit draft solutions for public scrutiny and comment. Public debate alone insures thorough consideration of all aspects of a problem, and enduring public policy must be hammered out on the anvil of rigorous and lengthy public debate.

Third, the Court cannot fashion the compromise solution that is often the hallmark of the statesmen. It must decide in favor of one party or the other. Consequently, one side wins and the other side loses. Yet enduring public policy must be acceptable to all major groups in the community and inevitably involves compromise.

Fourth, a Court that acts as statesmen arrogates to itself legislative and/or executive powers. It thus violates the separation of powers and checks and balances principles implicit in the constitutional distribution of power among the branches of the national government. A branch that draws all powers unto itself and makes itself the branch of last resort is scarcely "the least dangerous branch," as Hamilton assured his readers the judiciary would be.[36] The statesman's claim that the rightness of his principles or values validates them is morally arrogant. The statesman's claim that his principles or values are valid because of their identity with the people's is unprovable. Moreover, the oft-repeated argument that the Court should be free to disregard specific prohibitions on power or to fashion imaginative grants of power because the people's values have changed proves too much. If the people's values have in fact changed, they may change the law through the legislative or amendment process. Only the people should choose the public policies that govern them.

VIII. Conclusion: How Will Craftsmen Insure the Triumph of the Rule of Law?

The rule of law and constitutionalism will survive only if judges act as craftsmen. In contrast to the judicial statesman, the judicial craftsman is neither arrogant nor a usurper. He may pour into those general principles and values abstracted out of the Constitution only such meaning as language, original understanding, or historical practice suggest. When a craftsman decides cases according to principles or values derived from the text and its original understanding, he defers to the democratic judgment of the people when they adopted the Constitution. The craftsman understands that the legislature has already determined the classifications, whose definitions the judge must respect unless they violate the Constitution. In that way the judicial craftsman insures the evenhanded and impersonal application of the law, which is the goal of the rule of law.

In that way, too, the judicial craftsman insures the triumph of constitutionalism. In a society dedicated to democratic individualism, constitutionalism is the indispensable handmaiden of the rule of law. It envisions that the people will determine the law that governs them but simultaneously subjects the exercise of that awesome power to restraints, to insure its responsible and just exercise. First, the Constitution diffuses power by requiring different bodies to agree before any law is enacted. Second, the Constitution imposes specific limitations on the power of government.[1]

The Court plays an essential role in enforcing both restraints. It must umpire the federal system, insisting that all players observe the rules. The Court must enforce respect for the federal principle. Otherwise, the states will lose their status as sovereign states in a sovereign union. They will be reduced to administrative units of the national government, obliged to execute policies decreed from Washington rather than fashioned in local councils and statehouses. The Court's failure to articulate a constitutionally based, judicially enforceable limitation on Congress's commerce clause powers has contributed immeasurably to the erosion of the federal principle. When the Court characterizes an enumerated power like the power to regulate interstate commerce as plenary and then fails to define the scope of that plenary power, it subverts the theory of limited government that the framers espoused. A government of limited powers of unlimited scope is a contradiction in terms.

The oft-repeated argument that the states can protect themselves through the political process because they are represented in the national government scarcely justifies the Court's abandonment of its umpire role. In the first place, each state, like each individual, is entitled to the protection of the Constitution. The Court should protect dissenting states from overweening congressional majorities just as zealously as it protects dissenting individuals from overweening popular majorities. The framers were especially sensitive to such fears, which were voiced repeatedly in the deliberations of the Constitutional Convention.[2] In the second place, the power of the states to protect themselves through their participation in Congress is exaggerated. Now that senators are elected directly by the people rather than by state legislatures, the average senator owes little loyalty to his state government and has no particular reason to guard against actions that will circumscribe its authority. Because he need not answer to the state legislature, he can—and does—ignore its interests.

Similarly, the Court must enforce the separation of powers and checks and balances principles. The framers vested *all* legislative powers in Congress, *the* executive power in the President, and *the* judicial power in the courts. While they did grant each of the branches powers by which it could check the exercise of vested power by the other branches, none of the checks envisioned that one branch would exercise the powers of the others. The Court once enforced this simple and fundamental constitutional principle through its antidelegation doctrine.[3] Under that doctrine it refused to permit one branch to delegate its powers to another branch or some other governmental entity. Unfortunately, the Court junked the antidelegation doctrine because its statesmen members decided that effective government depended upon an independent administrative bureaucracy.[4]

Having recognized that Congress enjoyed powers far broader than its members could ever exercise effectively, the Court gave its blessing to the creation of a new fourth branch of government: the administrative branch. Congress, by parceling its powers out among the ever-multiplying administrative agencies, at last could exercise its plenary powers fully. Once the Court removed its thumb from the hole in the dike, the dike broke and state governments were drowned in a flood of administrative regulations. Today's swollen national government bears no discernible relation to the limited national government created by the framers of the Constitution, and it is at least partially the creation of the statesmen who have sat on the Supreme Court.

Also, the Court must say no to governmental players when they want to do something that would violate those individual rights guaranteed in the Constitution. Players can exercise only that power allocated them, and they can exercise it only according to prescribed procedures. For example, a responsible Court would have decided *United States v. Korematsu*[5] differently. Korematsu was an American citizen of Japanese descent. In 1941 he lived on the West Coast. In the months after the Japanese attack on Pearl Harbor, fear grew that the Japanese might invade the West Coast. That fear, fueled by anti-Japanese sentiment, prompted military and governmental officials to demand the internment of all Japanese-Americans living there.[6] These officials imagined that many Japanese-Americans remained loyal to the Emperor and would transform themselves into a traitorous fifth column. They also worried that soldiers might be unable to distinguish the yellow-skinned, slant-eyed enemy from the yellow-skinned, slant-eyed patriot. They thus urged the President to relocate these American citizens to camps in the interior of the country. The President agreed.

Dissenting from the Court's affirmance of the military orders, Justice Jackson reminded his colleagues in the majority that their decision was a loaded gun with which a future President might kill democracy. Had the Court refused to sustain these relocations, it would have reinforced the pressure on any future President to respect the due process rights of American citizens. A Court that enforces those restraints thus serves the cause of liberty far more effectively than does a court that ignores them in unprincipled pursuit of ad hoc justice.

Judicial craftsmen and judicial statesmen do share a common faith. Both, for example, are committed to principled decision making because reason is the distinguishing characteristic of judicial judgment. Both also recognize that courts play a unique role in American society because they are charged with protecting the fundamental rights of the individual. At the same time both craftsmen and statesmen are basically skeptics.

This common ground conceals profound differences, however. Though both craftsmen and statesmen rely on principles to decide the case before them, they derive their principles from very different sources. Craftsmen look to the text of the Constitution, to the original understanding of that text, and to the historical experiences of the American people. Statesmen look to moral philosophy, political theories, and notions of the public good. The craftsman does not choose a particular principle; he finds it. What validates it as a principle for decision is its congruence with the values of the framers. The statesman does not find a principle; he chooses it. What validates it as a principle for decision is its wisdom and social utility. The craftsman searches for the right principle—right in the sense that the framers expected the Court to use it. The statesman looks for the best principle—best in the sense that its use will most effectively promote a just society.

Though both craftsmen and statesmen recognize that the courts play a special role in American society, they conceive that role very differently. The craftsman sees himself as a reluctant umpire who must occasionally tell the government that it has swung wildly and struck out. The statesman sees himself as an enthusiastic teacher who must prod and inspire the government to do better. A craftsman realizes that helpless minorities often have no recourse but to his court. He knows he must protect them from majorities that would deprive them of their constitutional rights. A statesman believes that he has broader obligations toward helpless minorities. He feels that he must maximize their opportunities to succeed. Thus the craftsman enforces the constitutional barriers against oppression of minorities. The statesman would tear down societal barriers to fuller participation by minorities.

Though both the craftsman and the statesman are skeptics, they are skeptical about different things. The craftsman doubts that neutral principles may be derived from sources independent of the Constitution. He doubts that their validity and wisdom can be objectively demonstrated. He doubts his capacity to foresee the future and to choose decisional rules that will facilitate its beneficial unfolding. By contrast, the statesman doubts that constitutional analysis will yield neutral principles. He doubts that such principles can be validated by reference to any intentions of the framers, and he doubts that their wisdom can be objectively demonstrated by the mere passage of time. He also doubts the capacity of representative institutions to anticipate and plan for a more beneficial future.

However much statesmen may be needed, they need not perform their work from the bench. However much the dream of the statesman may excite us, courts should not be burdened with its realization. Courts contribute most effectively to the development of a just society if their judges act as craftsmen. After all, at any given time the justness of any society can be debated, especially in its particulars. The just society is therefore one that is always in the process of becoming more just. The rule of law and constitutionalism make that process possible. Judicial craftsmen, for all their modesty, reinforce the rule of law and constitutionalism and thus maximize the possibility of a just society. Judicial statesmen, for all their confidence, undermine the rule of law and constitutionalism and thus minimize the possibility of a just society.

The Constitution cannot become just "what the judges say it is" if the rule of law is to survive. Justice Benjamin Cardozo (1932-1938) captured this truth succinctly when he wrote: "substitution...of [the judges'] individual sense of justice...would put an end to the reign of law."[7] If the rule of law is to survive, the Constitution must remain what the framers intended it to be—a statement of the fundamental and enduring principles of the American political regime.[8] The father of the Constitution reminded us that the only assurance that its powers would be exercised faithfully to those principles was adherence to the meaning as it was understood by the people who wrote and ratified it.[9] When Thomas Jefferson assumed the Presidency, he promised to respect the Constitution according to the safe and honest meaning contemplated by the plain understanding of the people at the time of its adoption—a meaning to be found in the explanations of those who advocated it.[10] And so must the Court. As craftsmen, they must defend the Constitution until the people change it.

NOTES

Introduction

1. 3C. Bowen, The Lion and the Throne 370-74 (1956).

2. Hart, *American Jurisprudence Through English Eyes: The Nightmare and the Noble Dream,* 11 Ga. L. Rev. 969 (1977).

3. Quoted in J. Bond & C. Rose, Introduction to Legal Skills 208 (1978) (unpublished materials).

Chapter I

1. The debate (into which Justice John Paul Stevens (1975-   ) subsequently entered) is composed of a series of public addresses delivered at different places and times. It is collected in *Addresses—Construing the Constitution,* 19 U.C. Davis L. Rev. 1 (1985).

2. *Id.* at 7 (address by Justice Brennan). Justice Brennan stated more traditional and conservative views at his confirmation hearing. 6 R. Mersky & J. Jacobstein, The Supreme Court of the United States Nomination 1916-72 at 40 (1975). (The Constitution may be altered only by amendment). In his speech Justice Brennan breaks the activist's vow of secrecy, which had prompted Judge Richard Posner to comment:

> Activists are ashamed to admit in public what they are about; they make you read between the lines. Although activism is respectable enough among academics today, it still is not sufficiently respectable among the general public for judges to dare to admit that they are activists; and this is the best evidence that judicial activism, 1984 model, is indeed unprincipled.

Posner, *The Meaning of Judicial Self-Restraint,* 59 Ind. L. J. 1, 18 (1983).

3. Marbury v. Madison, 5 U.S. (1 Cranch) 137 (1803).

4. Jefferson's Republicans made the first attempt: they sought to impeach and remove the Federalist Samuel Chase. Had they succeeded, they would have gone after John Marshall. *See generally,* Ellis, The Jeffersonian Crisis: Courts and Politics in the Young Republic (1971). As recently as the Nixon administration, Congressmen threatened impeachment of Justices Douglas and Fortas.

5. The Federalists first employed this stratagem in 1801, passing legislation that would have reduced the Supreme Court from six to five upon the first resignation or death of a sitting Justice. Thus, Jefferson would have been deprived of an early opportunity to ap-

point a Republican Justice. The most famous such stratagem was Franklin Roosevelt's 1937 proposal to pack the Court by appointing an additional Justice for every Justice who remained on the bench after age 70. *See generally,* Baker, Back to Back—The Duel Between FDR and the Supreme Court (1967).

6. The most famous instance was the Reconstruction Congress's act of March 27, 1868. It removed the Court's jurisdiction over a class of cases, including one—Ex Parte McCardle, 74 U.S. (7 Wall) 506 (1869)—that was *sub judice.* Congress hoped thereby to forestall judicial review of its Reconstruction policies. *See* Van Alstyne, *A Critical Guide to Ex Parte McCardle,* 15 Ariz. L. Rev. 229 (1973). In recent years hearings have been held and legislation introduced to restrict Supreme or federal court review of desegregation cases, abortion cases, and school prayer cases. *See generally,* Baucus & Kay, *The Court Stripping Bills: Their Impact on the Constitution, the Courts, and Congress,* 27 Vill. L. Rev. 988 (1982).

7. For example, Lincoln appointed Chase because he wanted someone who would vote to sustain the Legal Tender Acts. Jefferson appointed Johnson because he wanted a states' rights advocate on the bench. Roosevelt appointed Black because he wanted someone who would construe the Constitution liberally. Nixon appointed Burger because he wanted a law and order judge on the bench.

8. Cooper v. Aaron, 358 U.S. 1, 18 (1958) ("[T]he federal judiciary is supreme in the exposition of the law of the Constitution."). *But see* Jackson's message of July 10, 1832, vetoing the bill to recharter the Bank of the United States, 2 Messages and Papers of the Presidents 576, 581-3 (Richardson ed. 1896). Of *Cooper v. Aaron,* Professor Erler correctly states: "[It] utterly confounds the Constitution and the Court's exposition of it; in a word, it conflates the Constitution with constitutional law." Erler, *Sowing the Wind: Judicial Oligarchy and the Legacy of Brown v. Board of Education,* 8 Harv. L. J. Pub. Pol. 399, 407 (1985).

9. *E.g.,* Gibbons v. Ogden, 22 U.S. (9 Wheat.) 1 (1824) (Congress has plenary authority over interstate commerce); McCulloch v. Maryland, 17 U.S. (4 Wheat.) 316 (1819) (Congress may exercise unspecified powers in order to execute powers specifically delegated to it). *See generally,* Gunther, Toward 'A More Perfect Union': Framing and Implementing the Distinctive Nation Building Elements of the Constitution, Aspects of American Liberty—Philosophical, Historical, and Political (Corner ed. 1977).

10. The classic statements are found in the 1798 Kentucky Resolutions (authored by Jefferson) and the Virginia Resolutions (authored by Madison). Madison, for example, protested against the tendency of the "Federal Government to enlarge its powers by forced constructions."

11. Letter to William C. Jarvis (Sept. 28, 1820), 10 The Writings of Thomas Jefferson 160 (Ford ed. 1899).

12. *See generally,* C. Warren, 1 The Supreme Court of the United States in History 514-40 (1935).

13. Even Holmes ascribed much of Marshall's work to "the convictions of his party." O. Holmes, Speeches 90 (1913).

14. *See generally,* F. Frankfurter, The Commerce Clause under Marshall, Taney, and Waite (1937).

15. *See* Taney's opinions in Mayor of the City of New York v. Miln, 36 U.S. (11 Pet.) 102 (1837); The License Cases, 46 U.S. (5 How.) 504 (1847); and The Passenger Cases, 48 U.S. (7 How.) 283 (1849).

16. Dred Scott v. Sanford, 60 U.S. (19 How.) 393 (1856).

17. *See generally,* J. Alsop, The 168 Days (1973).

18. Panama Refining Co. v. Ryan, 293 U.S. 388 (1935) (code promulgated under NIRA unconstitutional); Railroad Retirement Board v. Alton Railroad Co., 295 U.S. 330 (1935) (compulsory pension program unconstitutional); Schechter Poultry Corp. v. United States, 295 U.S. 495 (1935) (NIRA itself unconstitutional); Carter v. Carter Coal Co., 298 U.S. 238 (1936) (Bituminous Coal Conservation Act of 1935 unconstitutional); United States v. Butler, 297 U.S. 1 (1936) (Agricultural Adjustment Act of 1933 unconstitutional).

19. *See* 4 The Public Papers and Addresses of Franklin D. Roosevelt 212 (1938).

20. For a thorough and provocative review of the Warren Court's jurisprudential romance with equality, see A. Bickel, The Supreme Court and the Idea of Progress (1970).

21. *See, e.g.,* L. Lusky, By What Right? (1975).

22. Baker v. Carr, 369 U.S. 186, 301 (1962) (dissent).

23. Shapiro v. Thompson, 394 U.S. 618, 677 (1969) (dissent).

24. *Compare* Lockner v. New York, 198 U.S. 45 (1905), *with* Williamson v. Lee Optical Co., 348 U.S. 483 (1955); *compare* Buck v. Bell, 274 U.S. 200 (1927), *with* City of Cleburne v. Cleburne Living Center, 105 S. Ct. 3249 (1985).

25. *Compare* United States v. E. C. Knight Co., 156 U.S. 1 (1895), *with* Wickard v. Filburn, 317 U.S. 111 (1942).

26. *Compare* Abrams v. United States, 250 U.S. 616 (1919), *with* Brandenburg v. Ohio, 395 U.S. 444 (1969).

27. *See, e.g.,* B. Siegan, Economic Liberties and the Constitution (1980); W. Berns, The First Amendment and the Future of American Democracy (1976).

28. Board of Education v. Barnette, 319 U.S. 624 (1943).

29. *Id.* at 646, 670 (dissent).

30. Griswold v. Connecticut, 381 U.S. 479, 507 (1965) (dissent).

31. *See* Trop v. Dulles, 78 S. Ct. 590, 608 (dissenting opinion of Justice Frankfurter):

> Rigorous observance of the difference between limits of power and wise exercise of power—between questions of authority and questions of prudence—requires the most alert appreciation of this decisive but subtle relationship of two concepts that too easily coalesce. No less does it require a disciplined will to adhere to the difference. It is not easy to stand aloof and allow want of wisdom to prevail, to disregard one's own strongly held view of what is wise in the conduct of affairs. But it is not the business of this Court to pronounce policy. It must observe a fastidious regard for limitations on its own power, and this precludes the Court's giving effect to its own notions of what is wise or politic. That self-restraint is of the essence in the observance of the judicial oath, for the Constitution has not authorized the judges to sit in judgment on the wisdom of what Congress and the Executive Branch do.

32. *E.g.,* H. Ball, Judicial Craftsmanship or Fiat (1978); Graglia, *Judicial Review on the Basis of "Regime Principles": A Prescription for Governance by Judges,* 26 So. Tex. L. J. 435 (1985).

33. *E.g.,* M. Perry, The Constitution, The Courts, and Human Rights (1982); Brest, *The Misconceived Quest for the Original Understanding,* 60 B.U.L. Rev. 204 (1980); Sandalow, *Constitutional Interpretation,* 79 Mich. L. Rev. 1033 (1981).

34. Judge Bork has said: " 'Are we all...at the mercy of legislative majorities?' The correct answer, where the Constitution does not speak, must be 'yes.' " *Neutral Principles and Some First Amendment Problems,* 47 Ind. L. R. 1, 11 (1971).

35. *Ibid.*

36. Chayes, *The Role of the Judge in Public Law Litigation,* 89 Harv. L. Rev. 1281, 1316 (1976).

37. *Ibid.*

38. Thus, Justice Black, who insisted that he was bound by the framers' text and their understanding of that text, construed the free speech clause broadly because he believed that the framers intended to forbid any and all governmental regulation of speech. As he was fond of saying, "no law" meant no law. Professor Martin Shapiro points out:

> [I]f neutral principles exist, activism or passivism does not lie in the discretion of the Justices. So long as constitutional decisions are viewed as simply the policy preferences of the Justices making them, then the Justices seem to be free to either give or not give an authoritative stamp to their prejudices. But if they have discovered neutral principles embedded in the law and the Constitution, there would seem to be a strong moral impetus to enforce them.

Shapiro, *Judicial Modesty: Down with the Old!—Up with the New?,* 10 UCLA L. Rev. 533, 540 (1963).

39. The phrase, of course, is Marshall's. McCulloch v. Maryland, 17 U.S. (4 Wheat.) 316, (1819). Professor Thomas Grey apparently takes the view that the framers intended the Court to interpret the "majestic generalities" in light of natural law principles. Grey, *Do We Have an Unwritten Constitution?,* 27 Stan. L. Rev. 703, 710 (1975). Professor Robert Sedler concludes: "Consequently, under Grey's view of original understanding noninterpretive review is legitimate because it is fully consistent with the intention of the framers that the Constitution embody both unwritten higher law principles and the textual limitations on governmental power." Sedler, *The Legitimacy Debate in Constitutional Adjudication: An Assessment and a Different Perspective,* 44 Ohio St. L. J. 93, 104 (1983).

Professor Sedler's conclusion does not necessarily follow from Professor Grey's assessment of the framers' intentions, however much Professor Grey may share it. Both professors apparently assume that natural law is an ever-changing collection of fluctuating principles rather than a set of immutable principles. Moreover, both apparently assume that those natural law principles are not incorporated into the text of the Constitution and therefore do not constitue a gloss on its meaning but, rather, constitute an independent body of principles separate and apart from the Constitution itself.

40. During the 1930's the debate was usually couched in conservative/liberal terms. In the 1950s the debate was couched in judicial restraint/judicial activism terms. Today the

debate is couched in interpretivist/noninterpretivist terms. The one disturbing trend is that the question has now become whether the Constitution should be interpreted rather than how it should be interpreted.

Chapter II

1. United States v. Butler, 297 U.S. 1, 62 (1936). Professor William Van Alstyne elaborates sympathetically on the Justice's statement, which is frequently ridiculed:

> As a concise summary of the judicial obligation, Justice Roberts' dictum is worthy of consideration despite the sophisticated criticism it obviously invites. To be sure, its comparison of the judicial task with a mere mechanical exercise may be subject to criticism; the thought that the judicial task is as simply done as laying down a T-square to see whether one line is perpendicular to another may itself not square even with an ordinary citizen's impression of the difficulty, to say nothing of those professionally involved in constitutional litigation. But the suggestion that the judicial task of constitutional review should be performed with the same undissembling interest in accuracy as one would bring to his or her own work bench is, nonetheless, a proposal of enormous and lasting appeal. In fact, it may capture more accurately than any other single statement exactly what most people would hope for from the Supreme Court.

Van Alstyne, *Interpreting This Constitution: The Unhelpful Contributions of Special Theories of Judicial Review*, 35 U. Fla. L. Rev. 209, 225 (1983).

2. *Justice Black and the Bill of Rights*, 9 Sw. U. L. Rev. 937, 938 (1977) (reprinted from a CBS News Special of Dec. 3, 1968).

3. Judge Posner dismisses the canons as "fig leaves covering decisions reached on other grounds." Posner, *The Meaning of Judicial Self-Restraint*, 59 Ind. L. J. 1, 5 (1983). He elaborates this theme in Posner, *Statutory Interpretation—In the Classroom and in the Courtroom*, 50 U. Chi. L. Rev. 800, 800-17 (1983).

4. Hurtado v. California, 110 U.S. 516 (1884).

5. *See, e.g.*, Marbury v. Madison, 5 U.S. (2 Cranch) 137 (1803); Gibbons v. Ogden, 22 U.S. (9 Wheat.) 1 (1824); and McCulloch v. Maryland, 17 U.S. (4 Wheat.) 316 (1819).

6. Sturges v. Crowninshield, 17 U.S. (4 Wheat.) 122 (1819) (Marshall, J.):

> [A]lthough the spirit of an instrument, especially of a constitution, is to be respected not less than its letter, yet the spirit is to be collected chiefly from its words . . . . [I]f, in any case, the plain meaning of a provision not contradicted by any other provision in the same instrument, is to be disregarded, because we believe the framers of that instrument could not intend what they say, it must be one in which the absurdity and injustice of applying the provision to the case, would be so monstrous that all mankind would, without hesitation, unite in rejecting the application.

7. The Federalist No. 37 (J. Madison) (Mod. Lib. ed. 1937) 229.

8. Indeed, one scholar has recently argued that the framers did not intend for anyone to revert to their original understanding. In an article as clever as its title, Professor H. Jefferson Powell contends that the framers expected that future interpreters of the Constitution would look solely to its language for its meaning. Specifically, he argues that they never intended future interpreters to ascertain its meaning from their original understanding of the Constitution's language. "The framers themselves did not believe such an interpretive strategy to be appropriate," he says. Powell, *The Original Understanding of Original Understanding*, 98 Harv. L. Rev. 885 (1985).

9. *Cf*. Grano, *Judicial Review and A Written Constitution in a Democratic Society*, 28 Wayne L. Rev. 1, 18 (1981).

> When a judge engages in interpretivist constitutional review, objective sources of judgment exist. Often. . ."the most important datum bearing on what was intended is the constitutional language itself." In addition historical events, legislative history, and the structure of the Constitution help inform the judge's...interpretational task.

10. Westin, *The Empty Idea of Equality*, 95 Harv. L. Rev. 537 (1982).

11. In his dissent in National League of Cities v. Usery, 426 U.S. 833, 862 (1976), overruled, Garcia v. San Antonio Metropolitan Transit Authority, 469 U.S. 528, 105 S. Ct. 1005 (1985), Justice Brennan invoked Justice Stone's dictum in United States v. Darby, 312 U.S. 100 (1941): "The [tenth] amendment states but a truism that all is retained which has not been surrendered."

12. *Cf*. Easterbrook, *Ways of Criticizing the Courts*, 95 Harv. L. Rev. 802 (1982) (original intentions rather than precedent should govern interpretation). *See also* Bennett, *Objectivity in Constitutional Law*, 123 U. Pa. L. Rev. 445, 474 (1984). ("[O]ver the years the judicial process will have given birth to an ever-expanding body of decisions, the ancestry but not much of the content of which will be traceable to original intentions.")

13. Wallace v. Jaffree, 105 S. Ct. 2479, 2517 (1985) (dissent). *See also* Snead v. Stringer, 454 U.S. 989, 998 (1981) (Rehnquist, J., dissenting). (Constitutional building blocks have been piled on top of one another so that the connection between the original provision in the Constitution and the [Court's] application in a particular case is all but incomprehensible.)

14. McCulloch v. Maryland, 17 U.S. (4 Wheat.) 316 (1819).

15. The late Justice Harlan frequently employed this approach. *See, e.g.*, his opinion in Poe v. Ullman, 367 U.S. 497, 542 (1961) (dissent). ("The balance of which I speak is the balance struck by this country, having regard to what history teaches are the traditions from which it developed as well as the traditions from which it broke.")

16. *Cf*. G. White, Earl Warren: A Public Life (1982) (Chief Justice Warren praised "for his own reconstruction of the ethical structure of the Constitution").

17. Baker v. Carr, 369 U.S. 186 (1962), and Reynolds v. Sims, 377 U.S. 533 (1964). *Contrast* McKay, *Reapportionment: Success Story of the Warren Court*, 67 Mich. L. Rev. 223 (1968), *with* Reapportionment in the 1970's (Polsby ed. 1971).

18. *See, e.g.*, Euclid v. Amber Realty Co., 272 U.S. 365 (1926); Agins v. Tiburon, 447 U.S. 255 (1980); Penn Central Transportation Co. v. New York City, 438 U.S. 104 (1978).

19. Planned Parenthood of Missouri v. Danforth, 428 U.S. 52 (1976) (state may not require spousal consent); Bellotti v. Baird, 443 U.S. 622 (1979) (state may not require parental consent); Akron v. Akron Center for Reproductive Health, 462 U.S. 416 (1983) (state may not require that abortion be performed in hospital).

20. Tushnet, *The Dilemmas of Liberal Constitutionalism*, 42 Ohio St. L. J. 411, 424 (1981): If Tushnet were a judge he would ask himself in each case, "which result is, in the circumstances now existing, likely to advance the cause of socialism? Having decided that, I would write an opinion in some currently favored version of Grand Theory [in constitutional law]."

21. Lerner, *Constitution and Court as Symbols*, 46 Yale L. J. 1290, 1294 (1937). ("Every tribe needs its totem and its fetish, and the Constitution is ours.")

22. Karl Llewelyn gave this view its classic statement in The Common Law Tradition of Deciding Appeals (1960).

23. Brest, *The Misconceived Quest for the Original Understanding*, 60 B. U. L. Rev. 204, 228-9 (1980).

24. Chayes, *The Role of the Judge in Public Law Litigation*, 89 Harv. L. Rev. 1281, 1316 (1976).

25. Wright, *Professor Bickel, The Scholarly Tradition, and the Supreme Court*, 84 Harv. L. Rev. 769, 797 (1971).

26. Bennett, *Objectivity in Constitutional Law*, 132 U. Pa. L. Rev. 445, 449 (1984). (Our conception of law and the duty owed to it does not envision judges in constitutional cases simply substituting their personal value judgments for legislative value judgments.) *See also* Leedes, *A Critique of Illegitimate Noninterpretation*, 8 Dayton L. Rev. 533, 543 (1983).

27. Wilkey, *Judicial Activism, Congressional Abdication, and the Need for Constitutional Reform*, 8 Harv. J. L. Pub. Pol. 503, 505 (1985).

Chapter III

1. United States v. Lee, 106 U.S. 196, 220 (1982).

2. *See generally*, R. Cunningham, Liberty and The Rule of Law (1979).

3. F. Hayek, The Road to Serfdom 54 (1944). ("[G]overnment is bound by rules fixed and announced beforehand—rules which make it possible to foresee with fair certainty how the authority will use its coercive powers in given circumstances, and to plan one's individual affairs on the basis of this knowledge.")

4. Mansfield, *Constitutionalism and the Rule of Law*, 8 Harv. J. Pub. Pol. 323, 325-26 (1985) (constitutionalism is indispensable to the modern rule of law).

5. *See generally*, F. Morley, Freedom and Federalism (1959).

6. The Federalist No. 48 (Mod. Lib. ed. 1937).

7. Myers v. United States, 272 U.S. 52, 293 (1926) (dissent).

8. *See generally*, F. Morley, *supra* n. 5.

9. The Federalist No. 48 (Mod. Lib. ed. 1937) 326. ("[A] mere demarcation on parchment of the constitutional limits of the several departments, is not a sufficient guard against these encroachments which lead to a tyrannical concentration of all the powers of government in the same hands.")

10. The Federalist No. 10 (Mod. Lib. ed. 1937).

11. The Orono, 18 F. Cas. 830 (C.C.D. Mass. 1812) (No. 10,5885). *See generally*, R. Newmyer, Supreme Court Justice Joseph Story 87-88 (1985).

12. NLRB v. Jones & Laughlin Steel Corp., 301 U.S. 1 (1937); Steward Machine Co. v. Davis, 301 U.S. 548 (1937); West Coast Hotel v. Parrish, 300 U.S. 379 (1937).

13. J. Knox, Experiences as a Law Clerk to Mr. Justice James C. McReynolds of the Supreme Court of the United States 670 (unpublished manuscript in the McReynolds collection at the University of Virginia).

14. McCulloch v. Maryland, 17 U.S. (4 Wheat.) 316 (1819). *See generally*, Catterall, The Second Bank of the United States (1902).

15. Strauder v. West Virginia, 100 U.S. 303 (1880).

16. *E.g.*, Brandenburg v. Ohio, 395 U.S. 444 (1969) (Klu Klux Klan speaker protected); Hess v. Indiana, 414 U.S. 105 (1973) (antiwar speaker protected); Bond v. Floyd, 385 U.S. 116 (1966) (civil rights speaker protected).

17. *Cf.* H. Phillips, Frankfurter Reminisces, 292-301 (1960).

18. *E.g.,* New York Times Co. v. Sullivan, 376 U.S. 254 (1964); NAACP v. Claiborne Hardware Co., 458 U.S. 886 (1982).

19. Letter to Bishop Madel Creighton (Apr. 5, 1887), reprinted in L. Acton, Essays on Freedom and Power 328 (1955).

20. Osborn v. Bank of United States, 22 U.S. (9 Wheat.) 738, 866 (1824). *See also* Home Bldg. & Loan Ass'n v. Blaisdell, 290 U.S. 398, 453 (1934). ("[T]he whole aim of construction as applied to a provision of the constitution is. . .to ascertain and give effect to the intent, of its framers and the people who adopted it.") (Sutherland, J., dissenting).

Chapter IV

1. *See generally,* Marcus, Truman and the Steel Seizure Case: The Limits of Presidential Power (1977).

2. *See* H. Truman, II Memoirs: Years of Trial and Hope 478 (1956). ("[The President] must always act in a national emergency.")

3. Youngstown Sheet & Tube Co. v. Sawyer, 343 U.S. 579 (1952).

4. *Id.* at 667 (dissent).

5. *Id.* at 679 (dissent).

6. *Id.* at 634 (concurring opinion).

7. *Id.* at 651 (concurring opinion).

8. *Id.* at 652 (concurring opinion).

9. *Id.* at 662 (concurring opinion).

10. Cong. Rec. April 9, 1959, at 3962-63.

11. Youngstown Sheet & Tube Co. v. Sawyer, 343 U.S. 579, 633 (1952) (concurring opinion).

12. *Id.* at 630.

13. *Cf.* J. Burns, Presidential Government (1966); *compare* W. Taft, The Presidency: Its Duties, Its Opportunities and Its Limitations (1916).

14. Youngstown Sheet & Tube Co. v. Sawyer, 343 U.S. 579, 640 (1952) (concurring opinion).

15. *Compare* Kauper, *The Steel Seizure Case: Congress, The President, and the Supreme Court,* 51 Mich. L. Rev. 141 (1952), *with* Corwin, *The Steel Seizure Case: A Judicial Brick Without Straw,* 53 Colum. L. Rev. 53 (1953).

16. Youngstown Sheet & Tube Co. v. Sawyer, 343 U.S. 579, 645 (1952) (concurring opinion).

17. *Id.* at 644 (concurring opinion).

18. *Id.* at 646 (concurring opinion).

19. *Id.* at 631 (concurring opinion).

20. *E.g.,* The Records of the Federal Convention of 1787 (M. Farrand ed. 1911). *See generally,* M. Farrand, The Framing of the Constitution of the United States (1913).

21. *E.g.,* Debates in the Several State Conventions in the Adoption of the Federal Constitution (J. Elliot ed. 1836).

22. Quoted in R. Morris, Witnesses at the Creation 259 (1985).

23. Youngstown Sheet & Tube Co. v. Sawyer, 343 U.S. 579, 641 (1952) (concurring opinion).

24. *E.g.,* Federal and State Constitutions, Colonial Charters (B. Poore, ed. 1877).

25. *See, e.g.,* B. Bailyn, The Ideological Origins of the American Revolution (1967).

26. *See generally,* Whiskey Rebellion (S. Boyd ed. 1985).

27. Youngstown Sheet & Tube Co. v. Sawyer, 343 U.S. 579, 612 (1952) (concurring opinion).

28. *Id.* at 615 (Appendix I).

29. *Id.* at 598 (concurring opinion).

30. *Id.* at 701 (dissent).

31. *Id.* at 660 (concurring opinion).

32. Bork, *Neutral Principles and Some First Amendment Problems,* 47 Ind. L. J. 1, 10 (1971). ("Courts must accept any value choice the legislature makes unless it clearly runs contrary to a choice made in the framing of the Constitution.")

33. Youngstown Sheet & Tube Co. v. Sawyer, 343 U.S. 579, 609-10 (1952) (concurring opinion).

34. *Id.* at 589 (opinion of the Court).

35. *Id.* at 588 (opinion of the Court).

36. *Id.* at 654 (concurring opinion).

37. *Id.* at 655 (concurring opinion).

Chapter V

1. 467 U.S. 229, 104 S. Ct. 2321 (1984).

2. *Id.* at 237, 104 S. Ct. at 2329.

3. Hawaii Land Reform Act (1967), Haw. Rev. Stat. 516 (1979).

4. 272 U.S. 365 (1926).

5. Berman v. Parker, 348 U.S. 26 (1954).

6. *Id.* at 33.

7. *Id.* at 32.

8. Hawaii Housing Authority v. Midkiff, 467 U.S. 229, 104 S. Ct. 2321 (1984).

9. *See generally,* R. Epstein, Takings: Private Property and the Power of Eminent Domain (1985).

10. Griswold v. Connecticut, 381 U.S. 479 (1965) (dissent).

11. Midkiff v. Tom, 702 F.2d 788 (9th Cir. 1983).

12. *Id.* at 791.

13. Letter from James Madison to Thomas Jefferson (Oct. 14, 1787), 5 The Writings of James Madison 29 (G. Hunt ed. 1900).

14. The Federalist No. 10 (Mod. Lib. ed. 1937).

15. 2 The Records of the Federal Convention of 1787 (M. Farrand ed. 1911).

16. 3 U.S. (3 Dall.) 386 (1798).

17. Midkiff v. Tom, 702 F.2d 788, 793 (9th Cir. 1983).

18. *Id.* at 797.

Chapter VI

1. The legal realists made this claim very early, of course. *See generally,* J. Frank, Courts on Trial: Myth and Reality in American Justice (1949).

2. *E.g.,* Tushnet, Following the Rules Laid Down: A Critique of Interpretivism and Neutral Principles 781, 793-96 (1983). ("The universal experience of historians, however, belies the interpretivists' expectations. Where the interpretivist seeks clarity and definiteness, the historian finds ambiguity.") *But see* Van Alstyne, *Interpreting* This *Constitution: The Unhelpful Contributions of Special Theories of Judicial Review,* 35 U. Fla. L. Rev. 209, 234 (1983).

3. *E.g.,* Brest, *The Misconceived Quest for the Original Understanding,* 60 B. U. L. Rev. 204, 214 (1980). ("[T]here may be instances where a framer had a determinate intent but other adopters had no intent or an indeterminate intent.")

4. A related though different criticism is that one can never understand the past in its own terms because one's analytical perceptions are infected with contemporary biases and preconceptions. H. Gadamer, Truth and Method (1975). *But see* E. Hirsch, Validity in Interpretation 245 (1967).

5. *Cf.* Sandalow, *Constitutional Interpretation,* 79 Mich. L. Rev. 1033, 1045 (1981). ("[A]ll the decisions shaping constitutional law to contemporary values can also be understood as coming within the general intentions of the framers. All that is necessary is to state those intentions at a sufficiently high level of abstraction.")

6. 3 Vanderbilt Alumnus 237 (June 1918) (speech by Justice McReynolds).

7. Meyer v. Nebraska, 262 U.S. 390 (1922).

8. *See generally,* N. Dawson, Louis D. Brandeis, Felix Frankfurter and the New Deal (1980).

9. Justice Brandeis consistently dissented from the Court's decisions invalidating New Deal legislation. *E.g.,* Railroad Retirement Board v. Alton Railroad Co., 295 U.S. 330 (1935); Carter v. Carter Coal Co., 298 U.S. 238 (1936).

10. Interview with Dr. Robert Lentz, Clinical Psychologist, November 15, 1985, Christie Clinic, Champaign, Illinois.

11. Judge Posner concedes that a particular personality type may be inclined to exercise judicial restraint:

> But a quite different type of personality or mind-set, the skeptical, might lead a judge to adopt a restrained posture—and did for example, in the case of Holmes and of Learned Hand. Skepticism may make a judge unenthusiastic about exercising power, because he lacks confidence it will do any good and therefore is unwilling to compete in the power arena with the other, thrusting branches of government.

Posner, *The Meaning of Judicial Self-Restraint,* 59 Ind. L. J. 1, 19 (1983). Not surprisingly, academic apologists for judicial statesmen counsel appointing a different personality type.

> [Justices should be appointed] who. . . are. . .capable of exercising noninterpretive review well. Noninterpretive review cannot serve the function I have attributed to it unless the Court is staffed by persons capable of subjecting established moral conventions to critical reevaluation—thoughtful, deliberate individuals not wedded to a closed morality, but committed to the notion of moral evolution and are themselves open to the possibility of moral growth.

M. Perry, The Constitution, the Courts, and Human Rights 143 (1982).

12. *See generally,* E. Levi, Legal Reasoning (1949).

13. 431 U.S. 678 (1977).

14. *Id.* at 717 (dissent).

15. L. Levy, Origins of the Fifth Amendments: The Right Against Self-Incrimination (1968).

16. *Cf.* Schmerber v. California, 384 U.S. 757, 779 (1966) (dissent).

17. L. Levy, *supra* n. 15 at 427.

18. *E.g.,* Schmerber v. California, 384 U.S. 757 (1966) (police may forcibly extract blood samples).

19. Charles Warren characterized the First Congress as "an almost adjourned session" of the Constitutional Convention. C. Warren, Congress, The Constitution, and the Supreme Court 99 (1925).

20. McCulloch v. Maryland, 17 U.S. (4 Wheat.) 316 (1819).

21. In the criminal context the Court has concluded that the sixth amendment guarantees an indigent the assistance of counsel at every "critical stage" of the criminal prosecution. *See, e.g.,* Wade v. United States, 388 U.S. 218 (1967). Profesor Sandalow has correctly pointed out that the framers intended no more than to insure that a defendant could have retained counsel. Sandalow, *Constitutional Interpretation,* 79 Mich. L. Rev. 1033, 1042 (1981). *See also* W. Beaney, The Right to Counsel in American Courts 27-30 (1955); F. Heller, The Sixth Amendment to the Constitution of the United States 109-10 (1951).

22. Matthews v. Eldridge, 424 U.S. 319 (1976).

23. *Id.* at 334.

24. Justice White had conceded this point in another context when he commented in an earlier opinion:

> Although the Court regularly proceeds on the assumption that the Due Process Clause has more than a procedural dimension, we must always bear in mind that the substantive content of the Clause is suggested neither by its language nor by preconstitutional history; that content is nothing more than the accumulated product of judicial interpretation of the

Fifth and Fourteenth Amendments.
City of East Cleveland v. Moore, 431 U.S. 494, 543 (1977) (dissent).

25. *E.g.,* Wallace v. Jaffree, 105 S. Ct. 2479 (1985) (dissent).

26. 452 U.S. 18 (1981).

27. *See, e.g.,* Bickel, *The Original Understanding and the Segregation Decision,* 69 Harv. L. Rev. 1 (1955).

28. *See, e.g.,* Bond, *Ratification of the 14th Amendment in North Carolina,* 20 Wake Forest L. Rev. 89 (1984).

29. *See, e.g.,* Bond, *The Original Understanding of the 14th Amendment in Illinois, Ohio, and Pennsylvania,* 18 Akron L. Rev. 435 (1985). *See also* E. Erler, Equality, Natural Rights, and the Rule of Law: The View from the American Founding (1984).

30. Regents of University of California v. Bakke, 438 U.S. 265 (1978).

31. United Steelworkers v. Weber, 443 U.S. 193 (1979).

32. Fullilove v. Klutznick, 448 U.S. 448 (1980).

33. Firefighters v. Stott, 467 U.S. 561, 104 S. Ct. 2576 (1984).

34. Regents of University of California v. Bakke, 438 U.S. 265, 407 (1978) (concurring opinion).

35. Vieira, *Of Syndicalism, Slavery, and the Thirteenth Amendment: The Unconstitutionality of "Exclusive Representation" in Public Sector Employment,* 12 Wake Forest L. Rev. 515 (1976).

36. Lemon v. Kurtzman, 403 U.S. 602 (1971).

37. M. Malbin, Religion and Politics: The Intentions of the Authors of the First Amendment (1978).

38. W. Crosskey and W. Jeffrey, Politics and the Constitution in the History of the United States (3 vol. 1953-80).

39. Kruse, *The Historical Meaning and Judicial Construction of the Establishment of Religion Clause of the First Amendment,* 2 Washburn L. J. 65 (1962).

40. *See generally,* M. Howe, The Garden and the Wilderness (1965).

41. *See generally,* D. Epstein, The Political Theory of the Federalist (1984).

42. That is precisely what one courageous federal district judge has held. *See* Jaffree v. Board of School Com'rs of Mobile Co., 554 F. Supp. 1104 (S. D. Ala. 1983) (states are free to establish religion in light of the original understanding of the first and fourteenth amendments). The Supreme Court reversed this judgment in Wallace v. Jaffree, 105 S. Ct. 2479 (1985). It described the district judge's conclusion as "remarkable" and rejected it on the basis of the Court's own precedents. The Court declined to refute the district judge's extended historical analysis, however.

43. The most obvious objection would be that preferential treatment violated the equal protection clause.

44. Van Alstyne, *Trends in the Supreme Court: Mr. Jefferson's Crumbling Wall—A Comment on Lynch v. Donnelly,* 1984 Duke L. F. 770.

45. *See generally,* Cord, *Church-State Separation: Restoring the "No Preference" Doctrine of the First Amendment,* 9 Harv. J. L. & Pub. Pol. 129 (1986).

46. 370 U.S. 421, 430 (1962).

47. United States v. Lee, 455 U.S. 252 (1982). *See* especially Justice Stevens's concurring opinion (there is "virtually no room for a 'constitutionally required exemption' on religious grounds from a valid tax that is entirely neutral in its general application").

48. *See* Gaffney, *Political Divisiveness Along Religious Lines: The Entanglement of the Court in Sloppy History and Bad Public Policy,* 24 St. Louis U. L. J. 205 (1980).

Chapter VII

1. Wilkey, *Judicial Activism, Congressional Abdication, and the Need for Constitutional Reform,* 8 Harv. J. Pub. Pol. 503, 516 (1985).

2. The Washington Post, June 2, 1983, at A-21.

3. Wilkey, *supra* n. 1 at 519.

4. Letter to Congressmen Hill (July 6, 1935) 4 The Papers and Addresses of Franklin D. Roosevelt 297-98 (1938).

5. A Congressman also takes an oath to support the Constitution.

6. Baker v. Carr, 369 U.S. 186, 270 (1962) (dissent).

7. M. Perry, The Constitution, the Courts, and Human Rights 128 (1982).

8. *Cf.* Wiseman, *The New Supreme Court Commentators: The Principled, The Political, and the Philosophical,* 10 Hastings. Const. L. J. 317, 388. ("Some commentators like Fiss reduce the Court to the status of just another political actor.")

9. Thayer, *The Origin and Scope of the American Doctrine of Constitutional Law,* 7 Harv. L. Rev. 129 (1893); H. Commager, Majority Rule and Minority Rights (1943).

10. R. Neely, How Courts Govern America (1981) (courts must play the role that representative institutions would play if they were not corrupt).

11. M. Perry, The Constitution, The Courts, and Human Rights 102 (1982). *See also* J. Choper, Judicial Review and the National Political Process 68 (1980) (only politically insulated courts can protect minorities from irresponsible political majorities).

12. Justice Jackson, presumably familiar with history, wrote that "time has proved that [the Court's] judgment was wrong upon most of the outstanding issues upon which it has chosen to challenge the popular branches." R. Jackson, The Struggle for Judicial Supremacy 37 (1941).

13. *See generally,* 2 Chafee, Free Speech in the United States (1941). *Compare* L. Levy, Legacy of Suppression: Freedom of Speech and Press in Early American History (1960).

14. *But see* Levy, Jefferson and Civil Liberties: the Darker Side (1963).

15. Dred Scott v. Sanford, U.S. (19 How.) 393 (1857).

16. Smith v. Allwright, 321 U.S. 649, 669 (dissent).

17. 426 U.S. 833 (1976).

18. Hodel v. Virginia Surface Mining & Reclamation Ass'n, 452 U.S. 264 (1981); United Transportation Union v. Long Island Railroad Co., 455 U.S. 678 (1982); FERC v. Mississippi, 456 U.S. 742 (1982); EEOC v. Wyoming, 460 U.S. 226 (1983). This series of cases is perceptively analyzed in Comment, *Garcia v. San Antonio Metropolitan Transit Authority and the Manifest Destiny of Congressional Power,* 8 Harv. J. L. Pub. Pol. 745

(1985).

19. 105 S. Ct. 1005 (1985).

20. *Id.* at 1016.

21. *Id.* at 1033 (dissent).

22. Hart, *The Supreme Court, 1958 Term Foreword: The Time Chart of the Justices,* 73 Harv. L. Rev. 84, 99 (1959).

23. Brest, *The Misconceived Quest for the Original Understanding,* 60 B. U. L. Rev. 204, 231 (1980).

24. Contrast, for example, Justice Powell's assertion in early affirmative action cases that innocent persons could not be made to bear the burden of remedying the effects past discrimination with his insistence in the most recent case that the imposition of such burden is inescapable.

25. Leedes, *A Critique of Illegitimate Noninterpretivism,* 8 Dayton L. Rev. 533, 539 (1983). ("Few (so-called) interpretivists suggest that the judges have the power to write on a clean slate.") Thus, noninterpretivists strain to demonstrate that the statesman is constrained by objective standards. *See, e.g.,* R. Dworkin, Taking Rights Seriously 149 (1977) (judge should fuse moral and political philosophy in his search for the "right" answer); M. Perry, The Constitution, The Courts, and Human Rights 102 (1982) (there are discoverable right answers to fundamental political-moral problems); J. Ely, Democracy and Distrust (1980) (representativeness in the political process is an overarching constitutional value that will guide judges to correct decisions).

26. *See* the excellent survey of the particular principles and values prized by the new commentators in Wiseman, *The New Supreme Court Commentators: The Principled, The Political, and the Philosophical, supra* n. 8 at 355-417.

27. Karst, *The Supreme Court, 1976 Term Foreword: Equal Citizenship Under the Fourteenth Amendment,* 91 Harv. L. Rev. 1 (1977). Professor Karst would whet the Court's appetite for more principles should it find the principle of equal citizenship unsatisfactory or inadequate. He has also argued for a principle of "equal liberty of expression," Karst, *Equality as the Central Principle in the First Amendment,* 43 U. Chi. L. Rev. 20 (1975), and a principle of "freedom of intimate association," Karst, *The Freedom of Intimate Association,* 89 Yale L. J. 624 (1980).

28. Brest, *The Supreme Court, 1975 Term Foreword: In Defense of the Anti-Discrimination Principle,* 90 Harv. L. Rev. 1 (1976).

29. J. Ely, Democracy and Distrust (1980).

30. Professor Ely concedes that the judicial statesman in the end discovers only "his own values." Ely, *The Supreme Court, 1977 Term Foreword: On Discovering Fundamental Values,* 92 Harv. L. Rev. 5, 16 (1978). And Professor Brest concedes that even if "general principles can be found in social consensus or derived by moral reasoning, the application of those principles is highly indeterminate and subject to manipulation." Brest, *The Fundamental Rights Controversy: The Essential Contradictions of Normative Constitutional Scholarship,* 90 Yale L. J. 1063, 1067 (1981).

31. Fiss, *The Supreme Court, 1978 Term Foreword: The Forms of Justice,* 93 Harv. L. Rev. 1 (1979).

32. *Ibid.*

33. *See* Griswold v. Connecticut, 381 U.S. 479 (1965). *Compare* Note, *Roe and Paris: Does Privacy Have a Principle?,* 26 Stan. L. Rev. 1161 (1974), *with* Posner, *The Uncertain Protection of Privacy by the Supreme Court,* 1979 Sup. Ct. Rev. 173.

34. Judge Learned Hand pointed out that judges normally reflect the views of the class from which they come and to which they belong rather than the views of the whole community. K. Griffith, Judge Learned Hand and the Role of the Federal Judiciary 90 (1973). Professor Raoul Berger has elaborated on the point:

> Then too, as Leonard Levy bluntly stated, the Justices have run "from mediocre to competent," with very few distinguished exceptions—Marshall, Story, Holmes, Brandeis and Cardozo. The Justices, Alan Dershowitz, a former clerk to a Justice, wrote, "are generally mediocre lawyers, often former politicians. . .and almost always selected for the Court on the basis of political considerations." Although "we began with first rate men," Story told Kent, "we have now got down to third rate." John Quincy Adams, who knew many of the Associate Justices personally, said, "[n]ot one of them, excepting Story, has been a man of great ability. Several of them have been men of strong prejudices, warm passions, and contracted minds," a stricture later exemplified by Justices Peckham, Brewer and the Four Horsemen. Plainly, they were not better fitted than the people to "discover" what "moral evolution" required. Apart from such shortcomings, they have not been prepared, wrote a perfervid activist, Arthur S. Miller, "for the task of constitutional interpretation." Given the pressured life of successful corporate practice from which most Justices are drawn, it is too much to expect that they have found time to familiarize themselves with the basis and scope of judicial review, as their opinions reveal. "Few have," Miller states, the "broad-gauged approach and knowledge" essential "to search for and identify the values that should be sought in constitutional adjudication." In fact, the search "takes a different type of mind from that usually evident in the legal profession."

Berger, *Michael Perry's Functional Justification for Judicial Activism,* 8 Dayton L. Rev. 465, 480-1 (1983) (footnotes omitted).

35. Sedler, *The Legitimacy Debate in Constitutional Adjudication: An Assessment and a Different Perspective,* 44 Ohio St. L. J. 93, 137 n. 228 (1983).

36. The Federalist No. 78 (A. Hamilton) (Mod. Lib. ed. 1937).

Chapter VIII

1. Tribe, A Constitution We are Amending: In Defense of a Restrained Judicial Role 433, 441 (1983). ("The Constitution serves both as a blueprint for government operations and as an authoritative statement of the nation's most important and enduring values.")

2. Thus, it should come as no surprise that Madison wrote in Federalist No. 45: "The powers delegated...to the federal government are [to] be exercised principally on external objects, as war...and foreign commerce....The powers reserved to the several States will extend to all the objects which...concern the lives, liberties, and properties of the people, and the internal order...." The Federalist No. 45, (J. Madison) (Mod. Lib. ed. 1937) 303.

3. *E.g.,* Schechter Poultry Corps v. United States, 295 U.S. 495 (1935); Panama Refining Co. v. Ryan, 293 U.S. 388 (1935).

4. *E.g.,* National Cable Television Ass'n v. United States, 415 U.S. 336 (1974) (dissent). ("The notion that the Constitution narrowly confines the power of Congress to delegate authority to administrative agencies, which was briefly in vogue in the 1930's, has been virtually abandoned....")

5. 323 U.S. 214 (1944).

6. *See generally,* P. Irons, Justice at War (1983).

7. B. Cardozo, The Nature of the Judicial Process 136 (1921).

8. Erler, *Sowing the Wind: Judicial Oligarchy and the Legacy of Brown v. Board of Education,* 8 Harv. J. Pub. Pol. 399, 404 (1985) (court's role is to decide particular constitutional issues in light of the enduring principles of the American polity or regime).

9. 9 The Writings of James Madison 191 (Hunt ed. 1900).

10. 4 Debates in the Several State Conventions on the Adoption of the Federal Constitution 446 (J. Elliot ed. 1836).